Gems of Wisdom Heart of Gold

Inspiration from the past for people of the future

Javed Mohammed

Foreword by: Professor Sulayman S. Nyang

Pyramid Connections
Milpitas, CA
USA

45 S. Park Victoria, PMB 235
Milpitas, CA95035
USA

E-mail: gems1_us@yahoo.com
Website: gems.faithweb.com

Publisher has in good faith taken all reasonable care in the preparation of this book. For acknowledgements of works reprinted by permission please refer to the end of this book. Other referenced material is quoted under "fair-use" practice of the copyright laws and is copyright of respective publications. Some quoted material's source is unknown and publisher will be happy to put reference in subsequent revisions if so identified.

Library of Congress Preassigned
Catalog Card No.: 00 091403
Revision 1.0
ISBN 0-9701261-0-7

Printed in the United States of America

Gems

Acknowledgements

All praise is to the one and only God, Allah who makes things possible through his creation. Thanks to Farhad Amir, Dr. Ahmed Bangura, Dr. Mohammed Auwal, Dr. Dawood Sander, and Dr. Mujtaba Ghouse for their reviews and feedback of the manuscript. Special thanks to Dr. Sulayman Nyang for reviewing the manuscript and writing a touching foreword . Also the 1999/2000 high school students of Br. William (Isaa) Shandor of Granada Islamic School and the students of the senior class of the MCA Sunday School for their input and reviews. Thanks to Shaykh Mumtazul Haq of Milpitas, for ensuring that my content did not overstep any boundary. No book is complete without an editor and graphic designer so special thanks also to Ali Asadullah for doing the editing and Dino Azarcon for the graphics and layout. Also, many thanks to my parents and the rest of my loving family and to all those whose past efforts made this work possible. May Allah reward you all and make this a source of perpetual rewards.

Table of Contents

Gems

Gems

Gems

Gems

Foreword

American Muslims are beginning to make significant breakthroughs in the American Society. Evidence for this claim is the greater coverage of Muslim affairs in the American press and the recognition of their presence by government and religious leaders in the larger society. But if these Muslims are going to participate more effectively and responsibly in all the affairs of the society their intellectual presence must be affirmed and asserted. How can they do this? Well, the quickest and most effective way are for them to write their ideas down and share them with members of their multi-religious and multicultural society. By sharing the contents of their minds and by affirming their Muslim American identity through works like this one, they will soon gain favorable mention among non-Muslims who are presently woefully ignorant about Muslims. American society needs to know more about the Muslims and the best way for them to know this community is through its literature and culture. The sayings of great men and women of Islamic history can come to the attention of Americans only when Muslims themselves share their thoughts with and tell their values to their American neighbors. By combining the words of wisdom of great men and women of Islamic history with those of more familiar names listed in Quotable Quotes, American Muslims will gradually make their intellectual heritage part of the larger American mosaic.

This book by Javed Mohammed is one step in that long journey of Muslim recognition in the American social universe. What is remarkable about this collection is the interesting combination of biographical fragments with elements drawn from the rich experiences of human beings in many other cultures. Not only are young Muslims in North America invited to share the contents of their own life experiences, but they are also given a guided tour of the mental estates of Muslim heroes in Islamic history. Drawing from this harvest of quotes and from the words of wisdom from the Holy Prophet Muhammad and his Companions, including Ali Ibn Abi Talib, Mr. Mohammed hope to expose these young Muslims to the wisdom and wit of our spiritual ancestors. The materials contained in this book deserve our attention. Those youth who read widely will definitely come across familiar quotes here and there.

However, despite one's reading habit, the fact remains that this book adds to our youth's greater understanding of their heritage. Those who are not Muslims can also benefit from the materials presented. As a collection of quotes and statements of wisdom and wit from the library of human thought this book is a significant beginning for the Muslim compiler of quotable quotes for the enrichment of both the young and the old in the United States of America and beyond.

Professor Sulayman S. Nyang
Howard University
Washington, D.C. 20059
May 2, 2000

Where are we in our lives? Where have we been? Where are we headed? Having crossed the millennium as well as the middle age of forty — arbitrary marker of time but nevertheless significant milestones — has spurred me to reflect on such questions. I am not a historian or a scientist; nor am I rich or famous, but I do have some experiences I would like to share and pass on.

Being in Silicon Valley, moving at Internet time at the dawn of the Information Age when long-held beliefs and principles are being turned upside down and inside out, leaves many of us longing for something to cling to. Are there no more constants in life? Something far beyond the material pleasures that an Internet Initial Public Offering (IPO) and its subsequent riches can bring? How does technology affect humanity, spirituality, and social order? What follows, I hope, is something refreshing to read, learn, and to reflect on.

My desire to embark on this project emerged from a yearning to pass to my children some of what I have learned through the course of my life. Interestingly, my father, who is now over the age of 65, has done exactly the same for me and my siblings. As I feel a much wider audience can derive benefit from such a work, I am sharing the treasures we've gathered over time as well as those for which we've had to dig deeper.

This book is a collection of sayings conveyed by Prophets, Sages, historical figures, and people like you and me. A greater portion of the content is from Muslims. It draws on greatspeeches, quotes, and letters given at auspicious occasions, frozen in time immemorial. In some way, those who delivered these words, captivated their audiences with what they said and how they said it, and in the process have given us plenty of food for thought.

I would also like to start a process of bringing fresh thought from scholars to our youth so that we not only learn from our history, but also apply it to the real-world problems of today. Along with this, I'd like to contribute what I can, both in terms of what I'd like to pass on as lessons in life and what's been passed on to me by my father in his quest to do what I'm also doing.

In conclusion, this book offers, for your reference, inspirational speeches, anecdotes, and letters. Some of you may think that this is just history, but remember, history is the fuel of the future. Those who have ignored the lessons it teaches are now but a distant memory of the past. So let each of us live in the present to learn and to teach; to leave the world in a little better place than we found it.

If there is any good herein, then all praise is due to God; and if there are any mistakes, they are mine.

Introduction

If each of us look back at life there are some distinct stages through which we have moved that have helped define who we are. These stages typically follow the life cycle of birth, growth, maturity and, yes, the dreaded decline, that ends with death. I think I've made it to a certain stage of maturity, although I still have growing to do. It is this maturity I hope to draw upon in conveying the message of this book.

By way of introduction, I would like to reflect on some of the defining stages in my life and the lessons that I have learned from them. I would also like to tie this in with what the reader can expect from the book .

It is generally accepted that the best teachers in life are one's parents. Following parents in descending order of influence are family, friends, schoolteachers and other role models. I would like to reflect a little on some of them by starting with my grandparents.

Coming from farming communities, my grandparents and their forefathers were illiterate; yet they were people of high standing and dignity; their level of empathy astounds me. I heard from my grandfather that so as not to make life difficult for the poorer people by "raising the bar", they would give gifts so that no one would feel they were being stretched to match the gifts of well off people They would travel by foot using the stars for navigation. Clothes and food were simple. Muslims who were mainly peasants lived in harmony with the Hindus who ran the businesses, acted as bankers and were highly educated.

My parents were born in India in the late 1920s in the rural Punjab province. One of my grandfather's objectives in life was to have my father educated so that he could read incoming letters and write the replies. With this privilege my father finished ninth grade. My mother only made it to second grade before she was pulled out of school to take care of her baby brother.

In 1947, when the people of India struggled for independence from the British, war broke out between India and the newly formed Pakistan. At the time India had a majority Hindu and Sikh population, and Pakistan was to become the Muslim majority nation. My parents being Muslim and on the Indian side of the border along with their families, had to flee their homes, desert their lands, and abandon their prized animals. They would then face many weeks of travel by foot and ox-cart towards the border of Pakistan. Along the way, they endured floods, the plague and bandits who often slaughtered the men-folk and took the women. But Allah was, and has always been very kind; and my family, although coming so close to facing such hardships and atrocities survived.

I do not raise these memories for the sake of gaining sympathy; but, rather to show that the pains and struggle of the past have a certain universality. From Chechnya to Bosnia, and from Kosovo to Kashmir similar pains have been endured. So while we live in the comfort of our homes, we must not forget those who are in need of our prayers, personal help and our pocket books.

My father and mother were married in the fifties. My father is a very strong and disciplined man, just like my grandfather before him. Whether it be family or friends, all were awed by his presence. Timeliness and trustworthiness were two of his traits. My mother on the other hand was the softer compassionate type. Tolerance and patience are two of my mother's strongest virtues and those have paid her and our family dividends. Together my parents are the yin and yang of complimentary pairs. They lived simple lives off the salary my father earned working for Pakistan's Department of Forestry. Both my elder sister and I were born in Pakistan.

I was born in the spring of 1960. A few months later I was struck with what I would find out later was polio. Thanks to God I survived and was later able to lead a normal life. In 1961, my father emigrated to the UK. His story is almost like that of Dick Withington thinking that London was paved with gold. Except in his case, he went to Manchester expecting to see an enchanted place with the wizzardry of the industrial revolution. Instead he found a place where the sun was rarely seen due to smog and sighting the moon was a cause of celebration. His working life would start as a laborer. My mother, sister and I followed my father to England in 1964.

Whenever I ask my father about the major lessons of life, he always starts with his first job in the UK. The shock he got from the type of menial jobs he had to do as a train cleaner was severe. Jobs such as these were relegated to people lower on the totem pole back in Pakistan/India. Most of his working life, my father worked either night shift or early and late shifts as a bus conductor/driver. He says that moving to England effectively brought him down from his ivory tower and taught him about humanity.

To help my sister and I adjust to life in the UK, my parents provided us with a tutor, Abdul Haye (RA), who dedicated his services to the community for free. If I had to point to someone that exemplified selflessness and dedication, it would start with him.

Next in dedication comes my elder sister who acted in the maternal capacity, looking after her younger siblings when our mother was ill. Looking back it was a lot of responsibility for some very small shoulders.

We did not have a television in the 1960s, so any time there was something important to watch we would watch it at our neighbor's house in Manchester. Primarily, this used to be Muhammad Ali's fights back in the days of black and white TV. Our exposure to color TV first came in the 1970s. Once while visiting a family friend's house I got to see the Ali-Foreman title fight. I still, to this day, remember Muhammad Ali hitting Foreman so hard that a shower of sweat rained from Foreman's hair.

I must say that Muhammad Ali was indeed an important figure to me growing up. What made Ali so magnetic a personality to many of us was his dancing in the boxing ring and his talk and humor outside the ring. Whenever Ali won, he won for all of us Muslims; and when he lost, his loss was ours as well. Many publications in 1999, including USA Today, voted Ali as the Sportsman of the Century. Standing for principles and beliefs at the risk of losing popularity or material gain is what we learned from him.

Having been mainly a blue-collar laborer all his life, my father really got to appreciate the value of education. And the wake-up call of back-breaking labor was his incentive to strive to put his children through university.

I thank him for all that hard work, for it was through university life that I got to meet students from many parts of the world. The Muslims among them introduced me to another dimension of Islam, a pragmatic side that went beyond the ritual practices, bringing my "heaven and earth"

Gems

together.

Being a university graduate has allowed me and my family to reap the rewards associated with being a professional. It has allowed us to travel the world and to live in different cultures, most notably those found in Tokyo and Silicon Valley. There are a few lessons and one story I would like to share with you regarding these experiences.

First, I would like to emphasize that work can be very involving and can require all sorts of commitments and trials. To test the design of a computer I once worked on, I worked the night shift for several months. This was my first appreciation of the value of sleep at night versus day. It got me thinking about all those years my father had worked at night and slept during the day. It was very disorienting, for at times I was not sure of whether it was day or night, nor could I distinguish the day of the week.

Second, I would like to remind you that as we spend the majority of our lives chasing knowledge and wealth, we struggle to find the right formula for a successful life. I've asked many seasoned executives about this and one of the most common and interesting replies I received was: "No one says that at their death bed that they wish they had spent more time at the office."

So the question for us all is: What legacy will we leave behind? For no one will remember, after a few years, the car we drove, the neighborhood we lived in, the position we had or whatever material things we chased. It reminds me of the story of the tourist and the fisherman:

> A tourist goes to the beach and sees a fisherman
> laying in the sun with his fishing pole, waiting
> to catch a fish. The tourist, a businessman

from the city, asks the fisherman,
"Why don't you get a boat and go a little further
into the ocean so you can catch more fish?"
The fisherman asks, "And then what?"
The tourist says, "You can sell the fish, make more
money and get a bigger boat."
The fisherman again asks, "And then what?"
The tourist says, "You can sell even more fish,
make more money and get a fleet of ships".
The fisherman again asks, "And then what?"
The tourist, seeing that things have to come
to an end says, "Then you can sit back
and relax on the beach."
To this the fisherman responds,
"What do you think I'm doing right now?"

The moral of the story is that greed has no end, and the Prophet Muhammad (PBUH) has said that the Son of Adam will not be content even if he has a valley of gold, as he will desire another. So each of us should reflect on what we are doing and why.

In the dynamic times in which we live, during which change is constant, I believe that education — in order for it not to become stale — will have to be ongoing. That will keep it current throughout our working lives. This ties in well with the prophetic tradition of, "seeking knowledge from the cradle to the grave." But education and knowledge, of course, go well beyond work. Some of the greatest lessons pertaining to life I have learned, have been in Islamic classes taught by scholars like Imam Hamza Yusuf. Books, although they have their place, are no substitute for the interaction that takes place in a class. So take benefit from knowledgeable and righteous people around you.

Another life-defining event for me was my pilgrimage to Mecca, as I got to see and interact with people from every corner of the globe, all coming together for a common cause. One of the most memorable moments I have is standing at Mount Arafat with my father, who was making the most heart-warming supplications, the same place where Prophets from Adam to Mohammed (PBUT) had stood. I will leave it to Malcolm X's letter on the Pilgrimage experience to articulate the aura and feelings of this magnificent event.

Last but not least, my own children have taught me and shown me many things, including how different two individuals can be despite coming from the same parents. There is no Utopia, no ideal world. Reality has taught me that when one set of obstacles are overcome there's a new set waiting for us. As parents and individuals all we can do is our best and that is to a greater extent what this book and effort are about. What I have gathered for you in this book are, metaphorically speaking, just a few rocks. What you do with them, what you build from them and where life takes you, God only knows. I'll close with a story that bears relevance to what follows in the book:

There was once an African farmer who had heard how others had made fortunes finding diamonds. In his quest to become rich he sold his farm and spent his life looking for diamonds. Meanwhile the person he sold the farm to was one day passing by a stream on his land, where he saw something sparkle. When he put his hand in the water it appeared to be a translucent rock. He took the rock and put it on the mantle-piece. One day a geologist was visiting the new owner, and asked if he could examine the rock. It turned out that this was the largest uncut diamond that had ever been found.

One of the morals of the story is: that many times when you're looking for something it's right "under your nose". Had the previous owner taken the time to find out what a diamond was and where it could be found, he would not have wasted his life. So it is for me. Although I have circled the world many times over, the best treasures I have found have always been with me, especially the Qur'an and the examples of the Prophet (PBUH) his Sunnah. All that was ever needed was a key to unlock them.

And so it is with knowledge and wealth. Although getting an education and income are important, what is of greater importance is that we gain useful knowledge that benefits our lives; that we have wealth that allows us to fulfill our needs and helps those who are in need; that we have balance in our lives and can work for our livelihoods but also give time to our families and communities. I will leave it to the sayings of the Prophets, sages, and others to dwell on the subject. I hope the quotes and speeches will inspire you as they have inspired me. Read, Learn, Practice, and Pass-on for the benefit for all!

Chapter 1

Contemporary Collection of Wisdom

What follows first are the nuggets of wisdom my father, Ali Mohammed, has been collecting over the last ten years. He has told us that this is his legacy that bears more value than any material things he will leave behind. This is but a sample of what he has gathered and I have translated from the Urdu language. Unfortunately, I do not have the sources from where he gathered the gems. Some treasures are very poetic and do not translate well, so I have not included them. My own lessons are also included. For me this is an opportunity to reflect on both the values of the East and the direction we are heading in, in the West. Lastly, I share a summary of the lessons and important sayings I was able to gather from commencement speeches at high schools and colleges given my famous Americans from President Jimmy Carter to Marian Wright Edelman.

All that is shared has a common thread, a common yearning, and a common desire to pass on to the next generation what the school of hard-knocks has taught us. So I must say to the youth of tomorrow, "Do not repeat our mistakes, learn from them so that you also leave the world a better place than what you found.

Peace be with you!

Gems

1. Strive as much for this life as you're going to spend time in it
2. Strive as much for the hereafter as you're planning to spend time in it
3. Strive as much for the pleasure of Allah as you are dependent on Him
4. Sin as much as you have the strength to endure the punishment
5. Beg from one who is not dependent on anyone else
6. Disobey Allah only where you can hide from him (i.e. you cannot hide)

And More Gems

1. Every one who smiles at you is not a friend
2. The hardest thing in life is to counsel one self and the easiest is to criticize others
3. A true friend is one who comes your way when everyone else gives up on you
4. Those people are never successful who always are in need of support of others
5. Life is a journey, whose destination is death
6. Glance at the sky but don't forget that feet have to be kept on the ground

When Does a Person Remember God?

1. Student on the day of exam results
2. Poor when he's hungry
3. Rich when he's ill
4. King on seeing his kingdom disappear
5. One spouse seeing the other go astray
6. Parents on seeing their child turning to a failure
7. Criminal in the prison cell or at the point of execution
8. Passenger during turbulence on a plane

Ten Things That Consume Each Other

1. Goodness consumes wrong actions
2. Arrogance consumes knowledge
3. Forgiveness consumes sins
4. Lies consume provisions
5. Justice consumes oppression
6. Sadness consumes age
7. Charity consumes calamity
8. Anger consumes intellect
9. Backbiting consumes good action
10. Regret consumes wrong actions

Knowledge

1. Knowledge protects you, but you have to protect wealth
2. Knowledge without action and wealth without humility are useless
3. Knowledge without action is like the body without a soul
4. There are two types of knowledge; one that takes you to God and one that turns you away

Wise Sayings

1. Conquer your desires or your desires will conquer you
2. History tells us the loss of men in wars but who will tell the price paid by the women
3. Those who abuse time become the victims of time
4. Recognize a true friend who supports you not only in ease, but hardship

Advice of Three's

1. Keep control of three things: anger, tongue, and your dealings
2. Increase three qualities: stamina, love, and humbleness
3. Adopt three things: frugality, hard-work, and simplicity
4. Hope for three things: good health, good nature, and a good mind

I Love Those

1. Who establish prayer
2. Who strive (do jihad) in Allah's way
3. Who respect their teachers
4. Who revere their parents
5. Who spend in charity
6. Who gain knowledge of deen
7. Who like for others what they like for themselves
8. Who pass on the knowledge they gain
9. Who are simple
10. Who don't bow in front of anyone except Allah

Wealth

1. Wealth can only buy you some conveniences in life, beyond that it has little significance
2. Wealth is not made by how much you earn but by how much you save
3. Wealth can buy you beautiful ornaments but not good manners
4. Wealth can buy you books but not an education
5. Wealth can take your life but not give life
6. Wealth can buy almost everything except family (and friends)
7. Wealth can buy a comfortable bed but not sleep
8. Great amounts of wealth, power, and knowledge breed arrogance with the exception of a few
9. Money up to a point can improve your life. Beyond that you only have one stomach that you can fill, one bed you can sleep on, and one appetite. So think what you can do with your wealth, knowledge, power for the betterment of your family, community, and humanity at large.

Personal Lessons of Life

1. You don't always learn from your mistakes in life
2. Money and technology always run at a faster pace than the rate at which you chase them

Technology

1. The human touch will always outweigh the technical touch
2. In the end, technology including computers, networks, and the Internet are just tools. What you build with the tools is what counts
3. Consumerism is a zero sum game
4. Although the world is becoming digital a real part of it will always be analog
5. Getting megabits from a fast Internet connection is like drinking water from a fire hose. What counts is what's being communicated and what people do with that communication, not raw bandwidth
6. There's no getting away from politics, it's just some people are much better at playing the game
8. Ideas are a commodity, it's implementing them that makes a difference

World-Wide Social Problems & Islam

1. The only solution to the problems of both Muslims and non-Muslims is for all people to become aware of, understand and apply Islam in their lives
2. Islam has provided many safeguards against evil in every aspect of life that it nips them in the bud
3. Although the "movers & shakers" present Islam as an extremist religion, if you study it you'll find it is in the center. What is extreme and what is not lies in the mind of the beholder
4. To cure diseases of the mind and body, start with education
5. When you spend in God's way you get paid back in so many different ways
6. When the belief is one, goal is one, hearts are one, values are one then language or culture are small barriers to cross
7. The school of hard knocks is evolution not revolution for a peaceful change
8. The best of decisions are the ones you leave to Allah
9. If your gut feeling says something good, go with it
10. If something inside bothers you, leave it
11. Be a student and teacher for life, each enriches the other

Relationships

1. Lust appears in no time but love takes time to establish, so love just gets richer with time
2. You don't realize how much you pick from your parents until you're separated from them
3. Use the Midas touch with people but be careful what you ask for
4. Give unconditional love to children, family, and friends
5. Invaluable is the time and affection a mother gives to a child, so cherish the early years
6. Never be alone with a person of the opposite sex whose not related to you
7. Not everyone's going to be nice to you
8. As humans we're never immune from doing wrong. No matter where you are you're never alone and anything you say can be used as evidence against you
9. The true test of love or any relationship is when there are disagreements and challenges.
10. Marriage is a union of at least six people (man, wife and two sets of in-laws), so tread wisely.
11. Marriage can become your hell or your heaven on earth
12. Empathy and listening require a conscious, concerted effort which pays dividends in the long run
13. It requires a conscious effort to listen and not judge, to listen and not be readying your self for the rebuttal, to listen and not give advice without asking permission.
14. A lot of the time people just want to be heard
15. You can have many acquaintances but very few friends
16. Only emergencies need a quick fix, everything else needs time

17. Every person has a different path to success, however principles are in some shape or form the same
18. Admit your mistakes
19. Reduce the frequency of meetings with friends so that your friendship will last
20. Avoid junk food, junk news, and junk conversation. Be a person of real substance, and go beyond the superficial. Otherwise, nothing will be learned, nothing solved, and nothing gained

Present Day Truths.... Take the Time to Reflect

1. The paradox of our time in history is that we have taller buildings, but shorter tempers; wider freeways, but narrower viewpoints.
2. We spend more, but have less; we buy more, but enjoy it less.
3. We have bigger houses and smaller families; more conveniences, but less time.
4. We have more degrees, but less sense; more knowledge, but less judgment; more experts, but more problems; more medicine, but less wellness.
5. We have multiplied our possessions, but reduced our values.
6. We talk too much, love too seldom, and hate too often.
7. We've learned how to make a living, but not a life; we've added years to life, not life to years.
8. We've been all the way to the moon and back, but have trouble crossing the street to meet the new neighbor.
9. We've conquered outer space, but not inner space; we've cleaned up the air, but polluted the soul; we've split the atom, but not our prejudice.
10. We have higher incomes, but lower morals; we've become long on quantity, but short on quality.
11. These are the times of tall men, and short character; steep profits, and shallow relationships.
12. These are the times of world peace, but domestic warfare; more leisure, but less fun; more kinds of food, but less nutrition.
13. These are days of two incomes, but more divorce; of fancier houses, but broken homes.

14. It is a time when there is much in the show window and nothing in the stockroom; a time when technology can bring this letter to you, and a time when you can choose either to make a difference, ...or to just hit delete.

The above material is from an e-mail.

Gems

Lessons from Commencement Speeches

The following section covers the lessons I was able to distill from commemoration speeches given by contemporary figures, including President Jimmy Carter, Ben Cohen founder of Ben and Jerry's ice cream and Marian Wright Edelman, founder of the Children's Defense Fund[1]

1. People don't fit into boxes like pegs in a hole
2. You are just as good as anybody on the planet; but if you are going to succeed you will have to be twice as good as anybody else
3. You'll never make a good leader unless you learn to follow

&

Challenges of Life & Goals

1. No quest is worth taking that does not ask you to pass many tests and take numerous risks
2. Test to pass is not whether you fall down, but if you can get up after being knocked down
3. Life is never fulfilled, your journey over, until you take time to give back a portion of what has been given to you; so share what you have learned with others

&

Work & Career

1. Careerism is death. Don't confuse success with excellence
2. Give up addictions of all kinds
3. Your goals are your future, your past your guide
4. Insist on heroes and then be one
5. One action is better than a thousand conferences
6. Develop an inquisitive mind, know cause and effect, and you're world citizens
7. So learn about people and God's world. Ask yourself what will I do with my life, how can I be successful? And what is success?

Lessons in Life

1. Never work just for money (money will not save your soul, build a decent family, or help you sleep at night)
2. Don't confuse wealth or fame with character
3. Do not be afraid of taking risks or being criticized
4. Take parenting and family life seriously and insist those that you work for and work for you to do so
5. Never think life is not worth living or that you cannot make a difference
6. Remember what you love: when you remember what you love, you will remember who you are. If you remember who you are you can do anything
7. Appreciate the small triumphs throughout your lives. The great historic feats are rare, but the joy of life is made up of obscure and seemingly mundane victories

that give us our own small satisfactions, our own personal pleasures and our own momentary revelations[1]

Simple Lessons From Simple Quotes

Dream Your Dreams

• Enjoy the gift and privilege of life
• Envision Excellence
• Cherish and support your friends
• Give enthusiasm to others
• Be inspiring, know that you make a difference
• Take manageable risks
• Tell those that you love how you feel
• Live with passion
• Discover the gifts of daily life
• Aim for the stars
• Aim and radiate your love
• Recognize your inner beauty
• Think and live healthy
• Appreciate the good things in life
• Take pride in yourself
• Be greater than your highest thought
• Live your vision everyday
• Practice what you preach
• Appreciate yourself
• Live with integrity
• Think only the best of others
• Enjoy the journey

Make you dreams come true...

Take Time

1. Take time, it is the source of power
2. Take time to play, it is the secret of perpetual youth
3. Take time to read, it is the fountain of wisdom
4. Take time to pray, it is the greatest power on earth
5 Take time to love and be loved, it is a God-given privilege
6. Take time to be friendly, it is the road to happiness
7. Take time to laugh, it is the music of the soul
8. Take time to give, it is too short a day to be selfish
9. Take time to work, it is the price of success

Gems

Value of Time

- To realize the value of *one year*
  ask a student who has failed his exam.
- To realize the value of *one month*
  ask a mother who has given birth to a premature baby.
- To realize the value of *one week*
  ask an editor of a daily weekly.
- To realize the value of *one day*
  ask a daily wage laborer.
- To realize the value of *one hour*
  ask the lovers who are waiting to meet.
- To realize the value of *one minute*
  ask a person who has missed the train.
- To realize the value of *one second*
  ask a person who has survived an accident.
- To realize the value of *one millisecond*
  ask the person who has won a silver medal in the Olympics
- To realize the value of *one microsecond*
  ask a NASA scientist.
- To realize the value of *one nanosecond*
  ask a hardware engineer.

Gems

True Adjectives of Life

The following are narrations of the Prophet Muhammad (PBUH) that capture the essence of things in life.

1. True Success: The successful person is one who has accepted Islam, been provided with enough to live on, and has been made content by Allah for what He has given him.
2. True Wealth: Wealth consists of a variety of treasures, and those have keys. Blessed be whom Allah has made a key for good and a lock for evil, but woe to he whom Allah has made a key for evil and a lock for good.
3. The Reality of Life: A person may say "My wealth, my property." But his real property consists of only three things: What he eats, what he has worn and torn, and what he gives away (in charity) and so acquires. Everything else is left to others when he departs.
4. Focus on Life: Get a hold of five things before five things happen: your youth before your old age, your health before sickness, your wealth before poverty, your leisure before business and your life before your death.
5. Good Counsel: When you stand up for prayer, pray as if it were your last, don't say anything you will have to make an excuse for tomorrow and resolve to give up all hope of what people posses.
6. Allah's Blessing's: When you see someone who is better off than you, look at one who is not as well off as you. Doing this will keep you from despising the blessings Allah has given you.

7. Growing Friendship: Abu Hurairah used to visit the prophet (PBUH) everyday and spent much of his time with him. One day the Prophet (PBUH) said to him. "Visit me on alternate days so that our friendship and love might grow."

Miscellaneous Gems

1. A cynic is a man who knows the price of everything and the value of nothing.
2. Two men look out through the window, one sees the mud, the other sees the stars.
3. When the rich wage war, it is the poor who die
4. The hand that rocks the cradle is the hand that rules the world.
5. Farming looks mighty easy when your plow is a pencil and you're a thousand miles away from the cornfield.
6. Figure it out. Work a lifetime to pay off a house. You finally own it, and there's no one to live in it.
7. Youth is quick in feeling but weak in judgement.
8. Enough research will tend to support your theory.
9. Two things are opposed to reason; to spend more than what God has given us, and to die before the span of life granted by God has come to an end. "Whether offered up in gratitude, or uttered in complaint, destiny cannot be altered by a thousand sighs and lamentations."

Gems

Simple Principles

1. Live your life as an exclamation, not an explanation
2. Never invest or lend more money than you can afford to lose
3. Measure people by the size of their hearts, not the size of their bank accounts
4. Remember that a successful marriage depends on two things: finding the right person and being the right person
5. Learn to show cheerfulness, even when you don't feel like it
6. Everyday show your family how much you love them with your words, with your touch, and with your thoughtfulness
7. Be forgiving of yourself and of others
8. Evaluate yourself by your own standards, not someone else's
9. Acquire things the old fashioned way: save and pay cash
10. Don't use time or words carelessly. Neither can be retrieved[2].

Islam and Modern Science: Excerpts from MIT address by Seyyid Hossein Nasr

1. "When the West adopted Islamic science, it even adopted the gown of Muslim Scholars, but it never took the turban and put it on its head, ... we have taken both the gown and the cap from the West"
2. "Greek science was taken over by Muslims and Islamic science taken over by Latin West and later on by the European West. In both cases there was a period of transmission but there was also a period of digestion, ingestion, and integration which also means rejection. No science has ever been integrated into any civiliza tion without some of it being rejected"
3. "Gradually, Muslim governments are realizing that it's very important that if you have 100 students that you have 80 of them study science and technology but it's also very important that the other 20 study the humanities and to train some people in the history of science which altough allied to science is not really science itself. It is historical knowledge, it is linguistic knowledge and it is philosophical knowledge. The Muslims have not yet developed (but need to develop) their own hitoriography of science"
4. "Do not think that a science museum is simply neutral in its cultural impact. It has a tremenduos impact upon those who go into it. If you go into a building in which one room is full of dinosaurs, the next room is full of wires, and the third full of old trains, you are going to have a segmented view of knowledge which is going to have a deep effect upon the young personwho goes there,

who has been taught about tauhid, about unity, about the unity of knowledge, about the unity of God, the unity of the universe. There is going to be a dichotomy created in him. You must be able to integrate knowledge."

Sacrifice: Excerpt from The making of a Muslim by Khuram Murad

1. "Sacrifie means giving up things which are valued or desired. Those things may be tangible, countable like time, wealth or life, or intangible, unmeasureable like feelings, attitudes, opinions or aspirations. They are given up for the sake of something that is more worthy or more important or more urgent"
2. "Sacrifice is the stuff of which good and succesful, ordinary lives are made. Without it, life will be devoid of peace, harmony and cooperation, full of conflict and discord, a prey to celf centeredness, covetuosness, and immediate gratification of desires. Moreover, neither families nor communities can achieve cohesiveness and strength without some sacrifice on the part of its members. Also, no human endeavor can succeed in reaching its goal unless one sacrifices things valued or desired"
3. "Sacrifice is the nourishment without which the tiny seeds of iman will not grow into mighty, leafy trees, providing shade and fruit to the countless caravans of humankind.
4. "Without making sacrifices, the revival of Islam will always remain a matter of speeches or a matter of dreams. To actualize it, we will have to give up our time and wealth, our life and resources, our personal likes and dislikes. Even our best efforts, however, may not be perfect. We may waver and falter, we may fail and despair. But this is only human. What Allah looks at is our intention and effort. So let us turn to Him for help, lest our human frailties overwhelm us when sacrifices are demanded of us, and to

seek His forgiveness for all our shortcomings and failures.

Gems

Chapter 2

Wisdom: Divine, Prophetic & of Sages

The previous quotes and pearls of wisdom were contemporary advice for the era in which we live. However, I have found deep solace in the wisdom of old.

When I read what Luqman the Wise says to his son in the Holy Qur'an, I see myself saying the same to my son. The part of the story that really touches me is the verse which says that Allah has knowledge of even a mustard seed under a rock. It reminds me of a story I used to read to my daughter about a man, who has three sons. He gives each a piece of candy and asks them to go and eat it in a place where no one can see them. The two older boys eat their candy in different hideouts, but the youngest returns the candy saying that there is no place he could eat where Allah would not be watching. So the moral of the story is, of course, that none of our actions are hidden.

In terms of the sayings of the Prophet (PBUH), there is so much wisdom and practicality in them that I cannot articulate, in words their value. All I have done is capture a few samples, not only for their content, but also for their style. For example, the hadith on Charity builds from a series of questions and ends in such a powerful conclusion that we are left awed as to the value of charity.

While there are many hadiths on charity, one that really sticks in my mind and of which I have seen living proof, is: "Charity does not deplete your wealth." At a surface level, its meaning may not be obvious; but practically I have seen that whenever we spend in Allah's way, Allah gives to us in return from so many unexpected sources. So what follows is the advice of Prophets, Caliphs and Sages.

Luqman the Wise

Following is the wisdom and advice passed on by Luqman the Wise to his son, narrated in the Holy Qur'an. Timeless lessons for humanity.

We bestowed Wisdom on Luqman: "Show gratitude to Allah." Any who is (so) grateful does so to the profit of his own soul: but if any is ungrateful, verily Allah is free of all wants, worthy of all praise.

Behold, Luqman said to his son by way of instruction: "O my son! join not in worship (others) with Allah. For false worship is indeed the highest wrong-doing."

And We have enjoined on man (to be good) to his parents: in travail upon travail did his mother bear him, and in years twain was his weaning:

"Show gratitude to Me and to thy parents: to Me is (thy final) Goal.

"But if they strive to make thee join in worship with Me things of which thou hast no knowledge, obey them not; yet bear them company in this life with justice (and consideration), and follow the way of those who turn to me (in love): in the end the return of you all is to Me, and I will tell you the truth (and meaning) of all that ye did."

"O my son!" (said Luqman), "If there be (but) the weight of a mustard-seed and it were (hidden) in a rock, or (anywhere) in the heavens or on earth, Allah will bring it forth: for Allah understands the finest mysteries, (and) is well acquainted (with them).

"O my son! Establish regular prayer, enjoin what is just, and forbid what is wrong: and bare with patient constancy whatever betides thee; for this is firmness (of purpose) in (the conduct of) affairs.

"And swell not thy cheek (for pride) at men, nor walk in insolence through the Earth; for Allah loveth not any arrogant boaster.

"And be moderate in thy pace, and lower thy voice; for the harshest of sounds without doubt is the braying of the ass."[3]

Importance of Knowledge: Prophet Muhammad (PBUH)

It is narrated (by Mu'ath bin Jabal) that the Prophet Muhammad, peace be upon him, said the following:

Allah is great- There is no power except by Allah, the Most Elevated, the Great.

Acquire knowledge, for surely it leads to fear of Allah. Seeking it is an act of worship *(ibadah);* studying it is praising Allah; seeking it is jihad; teaching it to whomever doesn't know it is an act of charity *(sadaqah);* and giving it to its people draws one closer to them.

Knowledge points to the permissible (halal) and the prohibited *(haram);* and it is a shining light pointing the way to paradise *(jannah).* It comforts the lonely, befriends the estranged, and talks to you in seclusion. It is a guide through prosperity and adversity; it is a weapon against enemies; and it is the best of friends.

With knowledge, Allah raises people to high stations, making them leaders in goodness whose steps are traced. Their example is emulated, their opinion followed. The angels like to sit with the people of knowledge, surrounding them with their wings; and everything dry or wet-fish of the sea and animals on land-will ask Allah to forgive them.

For knowledge gives life to the heart in the midst of ignorance, and illumines vision in the darkness. With knowledge, God's servants become the elite and reach the highest degrees in this life and in the hereafter.

Contemplation with knowledge is equivalent to fasting (sawm); spending time to study is equivalent to standing at night in prayer *(qiyam);* duties to relatives are fulfilled by it; and through it the *halal and haram* are known. Knowledge precedes action *(amal)* and action always follows it. The fortunate ones attain it and the miserable ones are deprived of it.

Value of Charity:
Prophet Muhammad (PBUH)

When God created the Earth, it began to shake and tremble; then God created mountains, and put them upon the earth, and the land became firm and fixed; and the angels were astonished at the hardness of the hills, and said, "O God, is there anything of thy creation harder than hills?" And God said, "Yes, water is harder than hills, because it breaketh them?" Then the angel said, "O Lord, is there anything of thy creation harder than water?" He said, "Yes, wind overcometh water: it doth agitate it and put it in motion." They said, "O our Lord! Is there anything of thy creation harder than wind?" He said, "Yes, the children of Adam giving alms: those who give with their right hand, and conceal from their left, overcome all."

Prophet Muhammad (PBUH)

Al Targhib Wal Targhib
Tirmidhi and Baihaqi

The Affairs of This Life & the Hereafter

Khalid ibn El Waleed narrated the' following: A bedouin came one day to the Prophet (pbuh) and said to him: "o, Messenger of Allah! I have come to ask you a few questions about the affairs of this life and the Hereafter". (The bold letters are from our Prophet and the others are from the bedouin):

- **Ask what you wish.**
- I would like to be the most learned of men.
- **Fear Allah, and you will be the most learned of men.**
- I wish to be the richest man in the world.
- **Be contented, and you will be the richest man in the world.**
- I would like to be the most just man.
- **Desire for others what you desire for yourself, and you will be the most just of men.**
- I want to be the best of men.
- **Do good to others and you will be the best of men.**
- I wish to be the most favored by Allah.
- **Engage much in Allah's praise, and you will be favored by Him.**
- I would like to complete my faith.
- **If you have good manners, you will complete your faith.**
- I wish to be among those who do good.
- **Adore Allah as if you see Him. If you don't see Him, He seeth you. In this way you will be among those who do good.**

- I wish to be obedient to Allah.
- **If you observe Allah's commands you will be obedient.**
- I would like to be free from all sins.
- **Bathe your body from impurities and you will be free from all sins.**
- I would like to be raised on the Day of Judgment in the light.
- **Don't wrong yourself or any other Creature, and you will be raised on the day of Judgment in the light.**
- I would like Allah to bestow His mercy on me.
- **If you have mercy on yourself and on others, Allah will grant you mercy on the day of Judgment.**
- I would like my sins to be very few.
- **If you seek the forgiveness of Allah as much as you can, your sins will be very few.**
- I would like to be the most honorable man.
- **If you do not complain to any fellow creature, you will be the most honorable of men.**
- I would like to be the strongest of men.
- **If you put your trust in Allah, you will be the strongest of men.**
- I would like Allah to enlarge my provisions.
- **If you keep yourself pure, Allah will enlarge your provisions.**
- I would like to be loved by Allah and His messenger.
- **If you love what Allah and His messenger love, you will be among their beloved ones.**
- I wish to be safe from Allah's wrath on the Day of Judgment.
- **If you do not lose your temper with any of your fellow creatures, you will be safe from the wrath of Allah on the Day of Judgment.**

- I would like my prayers to be responded.
- **If you avoid forbidden actions, your prayers will be responded.**
- I would like Allah not to disgrace me oh the Day of Judgment.
- **If you guard your chastity, Allah will not disgrace you on the Day of Judgment.**
- I would like Allah to provide me with a covering on the Day of Judgment.
- **Do not uncover your fellow creature's faults, and Allah will provide you with a covering protection on the Day of Judgment.**
- What will save me from sins?
- **Tears, humility and illness.**
- What are the best deeds in the eyes of Allah?
- **Gentle manners, modesty and patience in adversity.**
- What are the worst evils in the eyes of Allah?
- **Hot temper and miserliness.**
- What assuages the wrath of Allah in this life and in the Hereafter?
- **Concealed charity and kindness to relatives.**
- What extinguishes hell's fire on the Day of Judgment?
- **Patience in adversity and misfortunes.**

Imam el-Mustaghfiri said: "I have never heard a tradition more comprehensive of the beauties of religion, and more beneficial than this hadith. It collects all the good things of Islam (Related by Imam Ibn Hambal). Editor's Note: It is my understanding that Angel Jibraeel (Gabriel) came in the form of the bedouin when the Prophet (PBUH) was with his companions so that they can learn the beauty of the great religion.

Caliph Umar's Advice

1. Do not be misled by someone's reputation.
2. Do not judge a person only by his performance of prayer and fasting; rather look into his truthfulness and wisdom.
3. One who keeps his secrets controls his affairs.
4. Fear the person whom you hate.
5. Prudent is he who can assess his actions.
6. Do not defer your work for tomorrow.
7. He who has no idea of evil can easily fall into its trap.
8. Judge a man's intelligence by the question he asks.
9. Less concern for material well being enables one to lead a free life.
10. It's easier to indulge in sins than to repent.
11. Contentment and gratitude are two great virtues; you should not care which one you are gaining.
12. Be grateful to him who points out your defects.

The Sayings of Imam Ali (R.A.)

Advice of Ali (RA), Companion and Caliph

Once Hadrat 'Ali took Kumail ibn Ziyad to a graveyard; when it was deserted, he heaved a deep sigh and said,

"Kumail, these hearts are containers, and the best of them are the most heedful of them. So remember what I am going to tell you. There are three kinds of people: One is the learned one who is godly; another is the learner who is on the road to deliverance. And then there are the uncultivated riffraff who follow every cawing, bending with every wind; they do not seek enlightenment by the light of knowledge, and do not resort to a reliable support.

Kumail, knowledge is better than wealth. Knowledge protects you, while you protect wealth. Wealth is diminished by spending, while knowledge grows by use.

Kumail, knowledge is a religion to which one is indebted; by it humanity acquires strength in life and beauty in speech when it has been fulfilled. Knowledge is the ruler, while wealth is the ruled.

Kumail, those who accumulate wealth have perished even though they are alive, while those with knowledge last as long as time; their individualities may be gone, but their example exists in hearts. Here (and he pointed to his heart) I have abundant knowledge, if only I could find people to bear it.

Unfortunately, I have found learners who are not faithful to it, applying it to the devices of belief in the world, gaining the upper hand over God's servants by means of the bounty of God, domineering God's friends by its authority; or those who find fault with bearers of truth without having any insight of their own. Doubt sparks in their hearts at the first sign of uncertainty.

Indeed, there is neither this nor that! Either they are greedy for enjoyment, submitting to the fetters of craving, or they are infatuated with collecting a hoard; neither type cares at all for religion, resembling freely grazing cattle in their ways. Thus does knowledge die out with the passing of its bearers. O God! Certainly the earth is not devoid of those who rise in honor of God for good reason, either openly and notably or in fear and obscurity, so that the proof and clarifications of God may not be in vain. But how many are they, and where are they? They are, by God, the fewest in number but the highest in rank with God. By them God preserves the divine proofs and clarifications until they entrust them to others like them and plant them in the hearts of others like them.

By them knowledge enters into real insight, and they are imbued with the spirit of certainty. They consider easy what seems hard to those who lead a life of comfort, and they take to what the ignorant are averse to. They are physically in the world, yet their spirits are suspended in the highest liberation. They are the deputies of God on earth, and are those who invite people to the religion of God. Oh, how I long to see them!"

The Sayings of Imam Ali (continued)

1. Associate with people in such a way that they weep for you when you die and long for you if you are alive.
2. The biggest failures are those who have failed to win friends, but even bigger failures are those who lose the friends they have made.
3. When little kindness comes your way, do not repel them by ingraitude.
4. Fear is linked to failure and timidity to deprivation and opportunity passes by like a cloud, so take a good opportunity.
5. The day of the oppressed against the day of the oppressor is more sever than the day the oppressor meets against the oppressed.
6. Love your friend with some reserve, for he might become inimical someday. Despise your enemy with some reserve, for he might become your friend someday.
7. How many lessons there are, and how little they are taken.
8. Hearts do advance and retreat, so when your heart advances, give it more to do, and when it retreats, restrict it to obligatory duties.
9. Your dignity is solid, but making requests evaporates it. So be careful about who it is before whom you allow your dignity to evaporate.
10. Praise that is more than deserved is flattery, while less than is deserved indicates incapacity of expression or else jealousy.
11. Do not say what you do not know, but neither say all of what you do know.
12. Remember, enjoyments pass while consequences remain.

Regarding Intellect

- A person's intellect becomes apparent through his dealings, and a man's character is known by the way he exercises authority.

- The intellect is a king and characteristics are its subjects, so if it is weak in governing them, disorder takes place.

- The intellect is better than desire, for the intellect makes you a king over your destiny, and desire makes you a slave of your destiny.

- Use your intellect to understand something when you hear about it-the intellect that examines, that is, and not just the intellect that repeats what it hears, for surely there are many who repeat the knowledge that they hear, and there are few who examine it.[5]

Speeches & Letters by Great Muslims in History

Style versus Substance

Here's a trivia question for you: Which President of the United States effectively won an election on a TV debate with a one-liner? Know the answer? Give up? It was Ronald Reagan. Want to know how? Read on.

I re-started writing this book, as the 1996 U.S. Presidential election was about to take place. Where else but in America would style be more important than substance? After all, you are what you wear in New York; you are what you drive in California, and you are what you eat and dress in Paris.

In the 1980 presidential race between President Reagan and Walter Mondale, the presidency was clinched in the second televised presidential debate between the two. Reagan was trailing in the polls after the first debate. Age was an issue for the President, in that if he were reelected, he would have become the oldest person to sit as President of the United States. In the second debate, however, Reagan used this one-liner: "I won't take advantage of my opponent's youth and inexperience." With that statement he turned a weakness into a strength, essentially won the debate and revived his campaign. The rest is history.

Similarly, in 1996 President Bill Clinton faced many criticisms related to ethics and morality. But once again perception won the day. Appearing presidential was the counter to criticism in that election and Clinton did just that and rose above the barbs tossed his way.

. To me, and I'm sure to many of you, substance is also integrally linked to style. As I have read the speeches and letters of some of the great Muslims in history, I have found that many address both style and substance. But it is the substance that has solidified their importance over time. I was mystified by the lack of substance and the nonexistence of educational material that would unlock the substance of Muslim discourse. Of course there are volumes of material covering western philosophers, leaders, and other great communicators. But as a Muslim, I find it surprising that Muslims who are recognized in the West as being influential in history, are not respected for the messages they brought to humanity at large.

Michael Hart, in his book, "The Worlds most Influential People" recognizes that Muhammed (Peace be Upon Him) was, in his opinion, the most influential person in the world. But despite the 1.2 billion people who follow Islam, when have you seen in Western literature, Muhammed or one of the great Caliphs, or even Muslims from the modern era being quoted? If Winston Churchill, Caesar, John F. Kennedy, Mao tse Tung, and Woody Allen can be quoted, why are people afraid of quoting the Prophet Muhammed, Omar the Great or Malik Al Shabaz (Malcolm X)?

Some might counter all this by pointing for example to the fact that a movie has been made about Malcolm X and books have been written about his life as well. However, I would argue that these are an anomaly.

Once I was in a presentation skills class, where we were asked to practice saying some lines of a famous person. When I mentioned I had selected Malcolm X, the instructor appeared very uncomfortable and suggested that I try

Winston Churchill instead. I had read a lot of Malcolm X's speeches and although those that dated from his time with the Nation of Islam contained racist elements, what I found of greater interest was the transformation that took place. After Malcolm visited Mecca he got to appreciate the universal nature of Islam. But the instructor was probably never exposed to or saw the worth of that.

Before we get into the speeches and letters, let me describe a term which helps to introduce the subject: the "East-brain West-brain." I was born in the East yet have spent most of my life in the West. I think each culture has made great contributions to humanity; and rather than see them as polar opposites I would like to expose you to some of the best speeches and letters from the Muslim world.

I start with Prophet Muhammad's last sermon as it addresses all the major challenges and guidelines we need to be aware of in life, all said in so few words. His qualities of speech are discussed as they lay the foundations for us of good communication. Also covered is his letter to Negus, King of Ethiopia. The Prophet Muhammad (PBUH) "builds a bridge between the two leaders" by stressing the commonality between Christianity and Islam.

Abu Bakr (RA), the first Caliph of Islam, is covered as his inauguration speech is so brief and full of modesty.

Next is Tariq bin Ziad, the commander of the Muslim army as it landed in Gibraltar en-route to Spain. The courage of a general to burn his ships and let his soldiers know there is only one way to go and that's forward is a remarkable event in history. His inspiring talk to uplift the moral and move his army is worth reading.

Next comes a statement by Al Mughirah to the Persian

Emperor Rustum. Here is a person addressing the leader of a superpower of the time with such fearlessness and clarity of objective and again in so few words.

Sayyid Ala Maududi is covered as a scholar of the last century with a moving address using a powerful analogy. Malcolm X is covered next with his letter from Mecca. As I have previously mentioned that seeing the transformation in this person take place from a race-based Nation of Islam to the equality taught and experienced by the followers of the religion of Al-Islam is incredible. A person, who lived and died a martyr for his beliefs, should be read and viewed in an objective way.

Muhammad Ali, I'm at a loss to describe in words a person with so many talents, speaking just being one of them. One who stood for his principles, at the expense of having his title stripped from him, but in all the times not saying a bad word of the people who instigated this. Patience, prayer and belief in God have again resulted in Muhammad Ali's contribution to society being recognized.

For a more detailed analysis of some of the speeches please refer to the Appendix.

The Prophet Muhammad's (PBUH) Last Sermon

"O People, lend me an attentive ear, for I don't know whether, after this year, I shall ever be amongst you again. Therefore listen to what I am saying to you carefully, and take these words to those who could not be present here today.

O People, just as you regard this month, this day, this city as Sacred , so regard the life and property of every Muslim as a sacred trust. Return the goods entrusted to you to their rightful owners. Hurt no one so that no one may hurt you. Remember that you will indeed meet your Lord, and that He will indeed reckon your deeds. Allah has forbidden you to take usury (Interest); therefore all interest obligation shall henceforth be waived.

Beware of Satan, for your safety of your religion. He has lost all hope that he will ever be able to lead you astray in big things, so beware of following him in small things.

O People, it is true that you have certain rights with regard to your women, but they also have right over you. If they abide by your right then to them belongs the right to be fed and clothed in kindness. Do treat your women well and be kind to them for they are your partners and committed helpers. And it is your right that they do not make friends with any one of whom you do not approve, as well as never to commit adultery.

O People, listen to me in earnest, worship Allah, say your five daily prayers (Salah), fast during the month of Ramadhan, and give your wealth in Zakat. Perform Hajj if you can afford to. All Mankind is from Adam and Eve, an Arab has no superiority over a non-Arab nor a non-Arab has any superiority over an Arab; also a white has no superiority over a black nor a black has any superiority over white except by piety and good action. Learn that every Muslim is a brother to every Muslim and that the Muslims constitute one brotherhood. Nothing shall be legitimate to a Muslim which belongs to a fellow Muslim unless it was given freely and willingly. Do not therefore, do injustice to yourselves.

Remember, one day you will appear before Allah and answer for your deeds. So beware, do not astray from the path of righteousness after I am gone.

O People, no prophet or apostle will come after me and no new faith will be born. Reason well, therefore, O People, and understand my words, which I convey to you. I leave behind me two things, the Qur'an and my example, the Sunnah and if you follow these you will never go astray.

All those who listen to me shall pass on my words to others and those to others again; and may the last ones understand my words better than those who listen to me directly. Be my witness O Allah that I have conveyed your message to your people."

Letter of Prophet Muhammad to Negus, King of Ethiopia

In the name of Allah, the Compassionate, the Merciful. From Muhammad (PBUH) Prophet of Allah to Negus, King of Ethiopia

I praise Allah, except who there is none to be worshipped, who is the Ruler of the world. He is innocent and pure (free from all blemishes, defects, flaws, or shortcomings). He gives refuge and sustains all.

I do admit that Isa (Jesus, PBUH) son of Mariam (Mary) was the soul from Allah and His word (order). He was infused to Mariam, who was clean and proof against evil. And Isa (PBUH) was born of Mariam. Allah created him from His soul and breath, in the same manner as He created Adam (PBUH) with His own hand. I invite you towards Allah the One who has no associate. Believe in Him, and join me in obedience to Him.

Follow me and accept my prophethood, because I am the Messenger of Allah. I have wished you well in conveying the message of Allah in all sincerity. It is up to you to accept my sympathetic advice. Extend the same invitation to your subjects. I am sending my cousin Jaffer (R.A.), with the other Muslims. When they reach you, treat them hospitably, by setting aside the vanity and pride of a ruler.

Peace is on him, who followed the right path.[4]

Other Speeches, Sayings & Lessons from Prophet Muhammad

(The following excerpts are taken from The Sealed Nectar)

First Speech of Prophet Muhammad (PBUH) to Pagan Quraish

"I celebrate Allah's praise, I seek His help, I believe in Him, I put my trust in Him, I bear witness that there is no god to be worshipped but Allah with no associate. A guide can never lie to his people. I swear by Allah, there is no god but He, that I have been sent as a Messenger to you, in particular and to all the people, in general. I swear by Allah you will die just as you sleep, you will be resurrected just as you wake up. You will be called to account for your deeds. It is then either Hell forever or the Garden (Paradise) forever."

Heart

The Prophet Muhammad's Style of Communication

The Prophet (PBUH) was noted for superb eloquence and fluency in Arabic. He was remarkable in position and rank. He was an accurate, unpretending straightforward speaker. He was well versed in Arabic and quite familiar with the dialects and accents of every tribe. He spoke with his entertainers using their own accents and dialects. He mastered and was quite eloquent at both Bedouin and town speech. So he had the strength and eloquence of Bedouin language as well as the clarity and the decorated splendid speech of town. Above all, there was the assistance of Allah embodied in the revealed verses of the Qur'an.

Hind bin Abi Halah: describes the Prophet Muhammad (PBUH) in the following way "The Messenger of Allah (PBUH) was continually sad, thinking perpetually. He had no rest (i.e. for long). He only spoke when it was necessary. He would remain silent for a long time and whenever he spoke, he would end his talk with his jawbone but not out of the corners of his mouth, i.e. (snobbishly). His speech was inclusive. He spoke inclusively and decisively. It was not excessive nor was it short of meaning. It was amiable. It was in no way hard discerning. He glorified the bounty of Allah; even if it were little. If he had no liking for someone's food, he would neither praise nor criticize.

When he pointed at a thing he would do so with his full hand-palm, and he would turn it round to show surprise. If he were angry he would turn both his body and face aside. When he was pleased, he cast his eyes down. His laughter was mostly smiling. It was then that his teeth, which were like hailstones, were revealed.

He never spoke unless it was something closely relevant to him. He confirmed the brotherhood relationship among his Companions; and thus he made them intimate and did not separate them or implant enmity among them. Those who were honorable with their peoples, were honored and respected by him and were assigned rulers over their own peoples. His cheerfulness was never withdrawn at anyone's face; even at those whom he warned his people from or those whom he himself was on the alert of. He visited friends and inquired about people's affairs. He confirmed what was right and criticized the awful and tried to undermine it. He was moderate in all affairs. He was equal to others and was not privileged. He would never act heedlessly, lest the others should get heedless. Each situation was dealt with in its proper due.

The Messenger of Allah (PBUH) was always cheerful, easy, pleasant tempered and lenient. He was never rude or rough nor clamorous or indecent. He was neither a reproacher nor a praiser. He overlooked what he did not desire; yet you would never despair of him. Three qualities he disposed of: hypocrisy, excessiveness, and what was none of his concern. People did not fear him in three areas: for they were not qualities or habits of his: He never disparaged, or reproached nor did he seek the defects or shortages of others. He only spoke things whose reward was Divinely desirable. When he spoke, his listeners would attentively listen casting down their heads. They only spoke when he was silent. They did not have disputes or arguments about who was to talk. He who talked in his presence would be listened to by everybody until he finished his talk. Their talk would be about the topic discussed or delivered by their first speaker. The Messenger of Allah (PBUH.) used to laugh at what they laughed and admired what they used to admire. He would always show patience with a stranger's harshness at talk. He used to say: "When you see a person seeking an object earnestly, assist him to get his need. And never ask for a reward except from the reward-Giver, i.e. Allah." (Ash-Shafi, 1/126)

Kharijah bin Zaid said: "The Prophet (PBUH) was the most honored among the people with whom he sat. His limbs could hardly be seen. He was often silent and rarely talked when speech was not a necessity. He turned away from those whose speech was rude or impolite. His laughter was no more than a smile. His speech, which was decisive, it was neither excessive nor incomplete.

Hadith Related to Communications

Anas (R.A.) has reported that the Messenger of Allah (PBUH) used to report his words thrice so that the meanings were understood fully, and whenever he came upon a nation he greeted its people. He would repeat salutation thrice (Bukhari)

Aisha (R.A.) has reported that the Messenger of Allah (PBUH) spoke distinctly so that all those who listened to him, understood him (Abu Dawud)

Ammar bin Yasir (R.A.) has reported that the Messenger of Allah (PBUH) as saying: To prolong the duration of Prayer and make the sermon brief indicate the intelligence of the person. Make your prayer long and your sermon short. (Muslim)

Abu Huraira (R.A.) has reported that the Messenger of Allah (PBUH) said: It is charity to utter a good word (agreed upon)

Lessons from the Hadith

- Excellence of using repetition and clear articulation to inculcate one's discourse into the minds of the audience
- Listening attentively
- Brevity in preaching
- Excellence of meeting people with a smile and politeness in speech

Abu Bakr's Inauguration Speech

Abu Bakr (RA) was the first Caliph of the Muslims after the death of the Prophet Muhammad (PBUH). He gave the following speech at his inauguration.

People! Even though I am not the best of you, I have been given the responsibility of ruling you. I will consider the weakest among you strong until I claim for them whatever is their due. And the strongest among you will I consider weak until I have taken from them whatever is due from them. O People! I am a follower (of the Prophet), not an innovator. So, if I do well assist me. And if I deviate, straighten me out. And reckon with yourselves before you are taken to reckoning.

No people ever abandoned jihad in the way of Allah except that Allah afflicted them with disgrace. And never did an obscenity appear among people except that Allah caused disaster to spread among them. Then obey me as long as I obey Allah! But if I disobey Allah or his Prophet, you owe me no obedience. I really prefer that another of you should have been given (and thus spared me) this responsibility. And if you expect me to assume the same role as the Prophet in relation to wahy (revelation), I cannot do that. I am only human, so make allowance for me[6].

General Tariq bin Ziad on Landing in Spain

Tariq bin Ziad is said to have addressed the Muslims with the following words:

"Where can you fly, the enemy is in your front, the sea at your back? By Allah! there is no salvation for you but in your courage and perseverance. Consider your situation: here you are on this island like so many orphans cast upon the world; you will soon be met by a powerful enemy surrounding you on all sides like the infuriated billows of a tempestuous sea, and sending against you his countless warriors, drowned in steel, and provided with every store and description of arms. What can you oppose to them?

You have no other weapons than your swords, no provisions but those that you may snatch from the hands of your enemies; you must therefore attack them immediately, or otherwise your wants will increase, the winds of victory may no longer blow in your favor, and perhaps the fear that lurks in the hearts of your enemies may be changed into indomitable courage. Banish all fear from your hearts, trust that victory shall be ours, and that the unbelieving king will not be able to withstand the shock of our arms.

Here he comes to make us the masters of his cities and castles, and to deliver into our hands his countless treasures; and if you only seize the opportunity now presented, it may perhaps be the means of your becoming the owners of them, besides saving yourselves from certain death.

Do not think that I impose upon you a task from which I shrink myself, or that I try to conceal from you the dangers attending this expedition. No: you have certainly a great deal to encounter, but know that if you only suffer for a while, you will reap in the end an abundant harvest of pleasures and enjoyments.

And do not imagine that while I speak to you I mean not to act as I speak, for as my interest in this affair is greater, so will my behavior on this occasion surpass yours. You must have heard numerous accounts of this island, you must know how the Grecian maidens, as handsome as *houris,* their necks glittering with innumerable pearls and jewels, their bodies clothed with tunics of costly silks sprinkled with gold, are waiting your arrival, reclining on soft couches in the sumptuous palaces of crowned lords and princes.

You know well that the Khalif 'Abdu'l-Malik ibn al Walid has chosen you, like so many heroes, from among the brave; you know that the great lords of this island are willing to make you their sons and brethren by marriage, if you only rush on like so many brave men to the fight, and behave like true champions and valiant warriors; you know that the rewards of Allah await you if you are prepared to uphold His words, and proclaim *His deen* in this island; and, lastly, that all the spoil shall be yours, and of such Muslims as may be with you.

Bear in mind that Allah the Almighty will select, according to this promise, those that distinguish themselves most among you, and grant them due reward, both in this world and in the world after this; and know likewise that I shall be the first to set you the example, and to put in practice what I recommend you to do; for it is my intention, on the meeting of the two hosts, to attack the tyrant Roderick and kill him with my own *hand, insh'Allah.*

When you see me bearing against him, charge along with me; if I kill him, the victory is ours; if I am killed before I reach him, do not trouble yourselves about me, but fight as if I were still alive and among you, and follow up my purpose; for the moment they see their king fall, these unbelievers are sure to disperse. If, however, I should be killed, after inflicting death upon their king, appoint a man from among you who unites both courage and experience, and may command you in this emergency, and follow up the success. If you attend to my instructions, we are sure of the victory!"[7]

Heart

Statement by Al Mughirah ibn Shubah to Rustum, Commanding General of the Persian Empire

Rustum suggested that since the Arab tribesman were moved to this war by their poverty and lack of food, the Persians would gladly give them wealth and food in plenty, provided they promised to return home.

Al Mughirah answered:

"We are here neither for food nor wealth, but to reorient your men from adoration of men to adoration of the one God. Our men are as eager to lay down their lives for this cause as your men are eager to preserve theirs. I call you to Islam. If you accept, you are one of us. If you do not, I offer you the peace of Islam and ask you to pay the *jizyah.* If you do not accept this, then war.

Cyrus, the archbishop of Alexandria and representative of the emperor who came to defend Babylon, returned to Alexandria after the fall of Babylon with the following description of the Muslims:

We have witnessed a people to each and every one of whom death is preferable to life, and humility to prominence, and to none of whom this world has the least attraction. They sit not except on the ground, and eat naught but on their knees. Their leader [Amir] is like onto one of them: the low cannot be distinguished from the high, nor the master from the slave. And when the time of prayer comes none of them absents himself, all wash their extremities and humbly observe their prayer.[8]

Heart

Has the Prayer Lost Its Power?

By Sayyid Abul Ala Maududi

Brothers in Islam! Undoubtedly you often ask yourselves: Why is it that the Prayer, good and beneficial as it is, seems to make no difference to our lives? Why does it neither improve our morals, nor transform us into a force dedicated to Allah? Why do we continue to live disgraced and subjugated? The usual answer will be that you are not offering the Prayer regularly or in the manner prescribed by Allah and the Messenger. Such an answer may not satisfy you. I shall therefore try to explain the matter in some detail.

Parable of the Clock

Look at the clock fixed to the wall, there are lots of small parts in it, joined to each other. When you wind it, all the parts start working and, as these parts move, the result appears on the clock face outside it which you observe. Both hands move to denote each second and each minute. The purpose of the clock is to indicate correct time. All those parts which are necessary for this purpose have been fitted together and the winding system has been made so that each of them moves as required. Only when all the parts have been assembled correctly and the clock wound up properly will it begin fulfilling the purpose for which it is made.

If you do not wind it, it will not show the time. If you wind it but not according to the prescribed method, it will stop or, even if it works, it will not give the correct time. If you remove some of the parts and then wind it, nothing will happen. If you replace some of the parts with those of a sewing machine and then wind it, it will neither indicate the time nor sew the cloth. If you keep all the parts inside the case but disconnect them, then no part will move even after winding it up. The presence of all the parts will not serve the purpose for which the clock is made because you will have disrupted their arrangement as well as their connection. In all these situations, both the existence of the clock and the act of winding it become useless, although an observer from a distance cannot say that it is not a clock or that you are not winding it. He will surely consider that it is a clock and will expect it to be useful as a clock. Similarly, when from a distance he observes you winding it, he will take it as a genuine effort on your part to do the job, hoping to notice the result which comes from winding the clock. But how can this expectation be fulfilled when what looks like a clock from a distance has in reality lost its 'existence'?

Aim of Muslim Ummah

Imagine Islam like this clock. Just as the purpose of the clock is to indicate the correct time, so the aim of Islam is that you should live in this world as the vicegerents of God, as witnesses of God unto mankind and as standard-bearers of truth. You must yourselves follow the commandments of God and bring all other people under Him:

You are indeed the best community brought forth for mankind: you enjoin the doing of right and forbid the doing of wrong, and you believe in God (Al'Imran 3: 1 10).

And thus We have made you a just community, that you might be witnesses unto mankind (al-Baqarah 2:143).

God has promised those of you who believe and do

righteous deeds that He will surely make you to accede to power on earth (al-Nur 24: 55).

And fight them, until there is no rebellion [against God], and all submission is to God alone (al-Anfal 8: 39).

Wholeness of Islamic Teachings

To fulfill this purpose, various parts as were required, like those of the clock, have been brought together in Islam. Beliefs and principles of morality; rules for day-to-day conduct; the rights of God, of His slaves, of one's own self, of everything in the world which you encounter; rules for earning and spending money; laws of war and peace; principles of government and limits of obedience to it - all these are parts of Islam. As in a clock, they are linked to each other in such a way that as soon as the winding is done, every part starts moving and, with the movement of all these parts, the desired result is obtained. Rule of God's law in the world, domination of Islam, start manifesting just as, with the movement of the parts of the clock in front of you, the time appears on its face.

In order to fasten together different parts of the clock, screws and small pieces of metal have been used. Similarly, to join all the parts of Islam together, there is an arrangement called the Jama'ah or organization. Muslims should organize themselves, and have leaders equipped with proper knowledge and endowed with taqwa; the brains should help them and the limbs should obey them, as they all strive to live under God.

When all the parts have been brought together and properly assembled, regular winding is necessary to set them in motion and to continue their movement: Salah which is offered five times a day provides that winding, creating the energy which sets an Islamic life in motion. Cleaning this clock is also necessary: fasting observed for thirty days a year cleanses hearts and morals. Lubrication, too, is required: Zakah is like the oil which is applied to its parts once a year. Then it is also necessary to overhaul it periodically: Hajj is that overhauling which should be performed at least once in a lifetime. And the more often it is done, the better.

Abusing the Clock

The processes of winding, cleaning, lubricating and overhauling are of use only when all the parts are present in the frame, when they are linked in the order designed by the clock-maker, and when all are so trained that immediately on winding they start moving and begin showing results.

Alas, today the situation has become very different. For a start, the very Jamah, the organizational structure, which was supposed to link the parts of the clock together has ceased to exist. The result is that all the fittings have come apart, each has gone its own way. Everybody does whatever takes his fancy. There is nobody to question anything. Everyone is autonomous. If someone wants to follow the Islamic code, he can; if he does not want to, he need not.

Since even this so-called freedom has not satisfied you, you have pulled out many parts of the clock and in their place put anything and everything: a spare part from a sewing machine, perhaps, or from a factory or from the engine of a car. You call yourselves Muslims, yet you render loyal service to Kufr, yet you take interest, you insure your lives, you file false law suits, your daughters, sisters and wives are forsaking Islamic manners and your children are being given secular materialistic education. Some have become disciples of Gandhi; others are following Lenin. Which un-Islamic gadget is there that you have not fixed into the frame of the clock of Islam?

Despite this, you expect the clock to work when you wind it! And you suppose that cleaning, lubricating and overhauling it will also be of use. With a little reflection, however, you should see that in the condition to which you have reduced the clock you can wind it, lubricate it, and overhaul it, for the whole of your lives without any effect. Nothing will happen until you remove the parts brought in from other appliances, replace them with the original parts, and restore the original priorities. Then, and only then, will the winding and so forth produce any results.

Why Worship Rites Are Ineffective

This state of affairs is the real reason why your Salah, Sawm, Zakah and Hajj make no impact upon your lives. First, there are so few among you who perform these acts of worship. Due to the dissolution of Islamic Jamaah everybody has become autonomous. Whether you fulfill your obligations or not, there is nobody to care. Nor do those who do apparently carry out their obligations do so in a proper manner. They are not constant in attending the congregational Prayer. People are selected to lead the Prayers in the mosques simply because they are fit for no other work: people who exist on the free bread doled out to mosques, who are uneducated, who lack moral calibre. How can congregations led by them turn you into the leaders of mankind? Similar is the situation regarding your Fasting, Almsgiving and Pilgrimages. Despite all these facts, you may argue, there are nonetheless many Muslims who do discharge their religious duties conscientiously. Why does that make no difference? But, as I have said, when the parts of the clock have become unhinged and numerous foreign bodies have been inserted in it, it makes no difference if you wind it or not, clean it or not, lubricate it or not. From a distance it does look like a clock. An outside observer may say: This is Islam and you are Muslims. But what he cannot see is how badly its inside machinery has been tampered with.

Condition of Muslims Today

To be slaves of the three idols, I say, is the real Shirk (idolatry). You may have demolished the temples of bricks and mortar, You may have broken stone idols in them, but you have paid little attention to the temples within your own hearts. To smash these idols is the essential precondition to becoming a Muslim.

This applies to all Muslims throughout the world. Whatever sufferings you are going through, I am sure, are the result of worshipping these idols. But because I am facing my Punjabi brothers here, I have particularly to tell them that the root of all their misery and humiliation is again precisely these three things. There are more than fifteen million of us in this land. But despite this we have no weight of our own.

Some communities numerically far smaller, carry much more weight. And what is the reason? It is solely by being slaves to our own selves, to family customs and to other human beings in preference to God, that our strength has been sapped from within. Let us look at ourselves. We have created among us many castes, like Rajputs, Gakhars, Mughuls, Jats and many others. Islam asked all these ethnic groups to become one Ummah, to be brothers and to unite harmoniously like a solidly-built wall of cemented bricks. But we are still clinging to the old pagan ideas. Just as there are separate castes among Hindus, so are we also split. We do not intermarry as Muslims should. There is no trace of brotherhood and fraternity between us. Verbally, we call each other Muslim brothers, but in reality we observe all those distinctions which were prevalent before Islam.

It is these distinctions which have prevented us from becoming a strong wall. Each and every brick in the wall is disjointed. We can neither rise together nor face any adverse situation together. If we are asked, in accordance with Islamic teaching, to break these barriers and become one again, what is our answer? Just the same as the opponents of all the Prophets gave: We cannot go against the customs which have come down from our forefathers. And, what answer was given by God to this obduracy? Only this: you do not have to break these customs and you do not have to give up following the rites of Hindus. But We shall break you into pieces and shall put you to disgrace and dishonor in spite of your large numbers.

Look further: Allah has commanded that your sons and daughters are both entitled to inheritance. What is your answer? 'No, for according to the custom of our forefathers, only sons and not daughters are entitled. We will follow the way of our forefathers in preference to the law of God.' Tell me, in the name of God, is this Islam? When you are asked to break this ancestral custom you say that you will break it only when others too break it. When asked why, you say because if others did not give a share to their daughters and we did, then we would be at a disadvantage when our sons took wives. Just consider what this reply means. Are we to obey the law of God only on condition that others obey it first? We shall be saying next: If others commit adultery, we shall also do it; if others commit theft, we shall also steal. In short, till such time as others give up sinning, we shall continue to commit sins.

In following your caste system and inheritance customs in such a manner all the three false idols we have been discussing are being worshipped. There is slavery to the self, to society, and to Kafir nations. And at the same time, while serving all these idols, we still claim that we nonetheless somehow belong to Islam! These are only two examples. We need only look at the situation with open eyes to see countless others. And in all these we will find that sometimes there is worship of one idol, sometimes of two, and sometimes of three. While these idols are being worshipped alongside the claims of allegiance to Islam and God, how can we expect Allah to shower His blessings on us - blessings which have been promised only to true Muslims?

Our Deplorable Condition

Brothers! You understand why it is so that you pray and fast and yet remain trampled under the heel of cruel tyrants. But, should I tell you something even more distressing? Although most of you no doubt regret this situation but, I would say, 999 people out of 1000 are not prepared to change their situation. They have no urge in their hearts to assemble the clock of Islam again properly. They are afraid that any such reconstruction would mean that their own favorite imported parts would be thrown out, and this they are not prepared to accept. They are afraid that any tightening of various parts would mean that they will have to discipline themselves, and this they are not willing to undertake.

Instead, they prefer that the clock remains a piece of decoration on the wall for people to be shown and told how wonderful Islam is, what miracles it can perform. Those who are supposed to love this clock more than others would like to wind it repeatedly and zealously and to clean it most laboriously; but they want to do nothing to reset its parts properly or tighten them, nor will they seek to get rid of the extraneous parts.

I wish I could endorse your attitudes and behavior, but I cannot say anything which I believe is wrong. I assure you that if, in addition to praying five times a day, you were to offer Tahajjud (predawn), Ishraq (post-sunset) and Chasht (mid-morning) Prayers, read the Qur'an for hours every day, and observe, over and above Ramadan, extra fasts for five and a half months in the remaining eleven months, you would still achieve nothing. What is needed is to restore the original parts to the clock and fix them firmly. Then even the little necessary winding will make it work smoothly; and the minimal amount of required cleaning and lubrication will be needed.

Wa ma 'alayn illa balagh. There is no responsibility on us except conveying the truth.

Letter From Mecca: Malcolm X

"Never have I witnessed such overwhelming spirit of hospitality and the true brotherhood as is practiced by people of all colors and races here in this Ancient Holy Land, the home of Abraham, Muhammad, and all the other Prophets of the Holy Scriptures. For the past week, I have been utterly speechless and spellbound by the graciousness I see displayed all around me by people of all colors.

"I have been blessed to visit the Holy City of Mecca. I have made my seven circuits around the Ka'ba, led by a Young Mutawat named Muhammad. I drank water from the Well of Zam Zam. I ran seven times back and forth between the hills of Mt. Al-Safa and Al-Marwah. I have prayed in the ancient city of Mina, and I have prayed on Mt. Arafat. "There were tens of thousands of pilgrims, from all over the world. They were of all colors, from blue-eyed blonds to black-skinned Africans. But we were all participating in the same ritual displaying a spirit of unity and brotherhood that my experiences in America had led me to believe never could exist between the white and the nonwhite. "America needs to understand Islam, because this is the one religion that erases from its society the race problem. Throughout my travels in the Muslim world, I have met, talked to, and even eaten with people who in America would have been considered 'white' - but the 'white' attitude was removed from their minds by the religion of Islam. I have never before seen sincere and true brotherhood practiced by all colors together, irrespective of their color. "You may be shocked by these words coming from me. But on this pilgrimage, what I have seen, and experienced, has forced me to rearrange much of my thought-patterns previously held, and to toss aside some of my previous conclusions. This was not too difficult for me. Despite my firm convictions, I have been always a man who tries to face facts, and to accept the reality of life as new experience and new knowledge unfolds it. I have always kept an open mind, which is necessary to the flexibility that must go hand in hand with every form of intelligent search for truth.

"During the past eleven days here in the Muslim world, I have eaten from the same plate, drunk from the same glass, and slept in the same bed (or on the same rug)-while praying to the same God-- with fellow Muslims, whose eyes were the bluest of blue, whose hair was the blondest of blond, and whose skin was the whitest of white. And in the words and in the actions and in the deeds of the 'white' Muslims, I felt the same sincerity that I felt among the black African Muslims of Nigeria, Sudan, and Ghana.

"We were truly all the same (brothers) -because their belief in one God had removed the 'white' from their minds, the 'white' from their behavior, and the 'white' from their attitude." I could see from this, that perhaps if white Americans could accept the Oneness of God, then perhaps, too, they could accept in reality the Oneness of Man-and cease to measure, and hinder, and harm others in terms of their 'differences' in color. With racism plaguing America like an incurable cancer, the so-called 'Christian' white American heart should be more receptive to a proven solution to such a destructive problem. Perhaps it could be in time to save America from imminent disaster-the same destruction brought upon Germany by racism that eventually destroyed the Germans themselves.

"Each hour here in the Holy Land enables me to have greater spiritual insights into what is happening in America between black and white. The American Negro never can be blamed for his racial animosity he is only reacting to four hundred years of the conscious racism of the American whites. But as racism leads America up the suicide path, I do believe, from the experiences that I have had with them, that the whites of the younger generation, in the colleges and universities, will see the handwriting on the wall and many of them will turn to the spiritual path of truth-the only way left to America to ward off the disaster that racism inevitably must lead to.

"Never have I been so highly honored. Never have I been made to feel more humble and unworthy. Who would believe the blessings that have been heaped upon an American Negro? A few nights ago, a man who would be called in America a 'white' man, a United Nations diplomat, an ambassador, a companion of kings, gave me his hotel suite, his bed. By this man, His Excellency Prince Faisal, who rules this Holy Land, was made aware of my presence here in Jedda. The very next morning, Prince Faisal's son, in person, informed me that by the will and decree of his esteemed father, I was to be a State Guest.

"The Deputy Chief of Protocol himself took me before the Hajj Court. His Holiness Sheikh Muhammad Harkon himself okayed my visit to Mecca. His Holiness gave me two books on Islam, with his personal seal and autograph, and he told me that he prayed that I would be a successful preacher of Islam in America. A car, a driver, and a guide, have been placed at my disposal, making it possible for me to travel about this Holy Land almost at will. The government provides air-conditioned quarters and servants in each city that I visit. Never would I have even thought of dreaming that I would ever be a recipient of such honors-honors that in America would be bestowed upon a King--not a Negro.

"All praise is due to Allah, the Lord of all the Worlds.

Sincerely,

El-Hajj Malik El-Shabazz
(Malcolm X)

Me . . . We by Muhammad Ali

The most recognizable man in the global village proves, once again, that he is the greatest.

"When you get to be 57, and you've been world famous and been called the greatest, met presidents and kings, and had books written about you, they ask you to write articles on subjects like convergence. Now, as I understand it, convergence means that society today is no longer pretending that there is any real difference between things like art and nature, science and religion, between the poetry a man makes out of words and the poetry God makes out of time and space, between the fight one man may fight for dignity in a ring and the fight a whole race of people may fight for dignity on the earth.

Athletes have always known this, from the first Greek Olympics to today's Special Olympics. Sports has to be the most convergent of all human activities because athletes know that there is no fundamental difference between body, mind, and spirit. To be truly great, an athlete must develop all three together, exercise them all together, and bring the strength of all of them to bear on the contest. Only then is greatness possible, and only then does victory have universal meaning because it reflects the fullness and richness of the human heart.

I wanted to be heavyweight champion of the world from an early age. I wanted it not only because it is the greatest title in sports but because the champion is a symbol of greatness itself—of what an individual can achieve through sacrifice, work, and faith.

But the title brings heavy responsibility: People all over the world look up to the champ, and whether he wants to or not, he becomes an example to them. Winning the heavyweight championship of the world is not just a great victory, it is a great duty. A man who seeks such greatness for money or other selfish reasons will never be able to inspire others. And a man who achieves such greatness and then is false to his own principles will have turned his victory into a lie.

I won the heavyweight championship for the first time in 1964, when I was 22 years old. I savored the overnight celebrity and basked in the media spotlight. Then almost at once I began to be challenged on my religion and then on my opposition to war. Those media spotlights quickly became interrogation lights, and the people who had celebrated me began ripping at me this way and that, demanding I support their stand. I very quickly found I had to decide what it really meant for me to be world champion.

It's hard to define yourself when you're young and at the summit of a vast and searching world. I had to look deep into myself for the answer.

Despite being champ, it was a lonely process, and before it was over, the title itself had been stripped from me, then won back, lost, and won back again. But what I gained was of much greater value.

As I look back on it today, I would say that what I gained was the ability to see the world in something like the way God must see it. To understand that there are no distinctions of any real importance in the affairs of men, that there is only one time and one place and one person and one truth. And that we are all contained in that time and place and person, and that the truth contains us all.

In our daily lives, we may find it convenient to make distinctions, to give numbers and names to things in the world, but that is like counting the drops in the ocean or classifying the leaves on a tree. The beauty of the ocean and the tree remains wondrous nonetheless, and filled with God's glory for the spirit and the mind and the fingers, young and old, that can reach out and discover it anew each day."

Muhammad Ali has captured the world's attention in many forms: as a three-time world heavyweight champion, civil rights proponent, draft resister, Olympic gold medal winner, and torchbearer at the 1996 Olympics in Atlanta.

How I'd Like To Be Remembered, Muhammad Ali

"I'll tell you how I'd like to be remembered: as a black man who won the heavyweight title and who was humorous and who treated everyone right. As a man who never looked down on those who looked up to him and who helped as many of his people as he could.... As a man who wouldn't hurt his people's dignity by doing anything that would embarrass them. As a man who tried to unite his people through the faith of Islam.... And if all that's asking too much, then I guess I'd settle for being remembered only as a great boxing champion who became a preacher and a champion of his people."[9]

Chapter 4

Sowing The Seeds

This chapter is about taking the inspiration from the past and start discussing practical ideas that we can all do. I defer to Shaikh Hamza Yusuf for his practical steps for changing our condition. To get the voice of our youth there is an essay by Maha Ezzeddine on the problems and solutions of the Muslim youth in America. Also a perspective on technology by the author.

Agenda for Changing Our Condition: Hamza Yusuf

Practical Steps for Changing Our Condition

- Form a serious study group to learn the five pillars properly and thoroughly.
- Create an active *dawa* program designed to produce results.
- Find an area of concern that instills a passionate response in you and begin to work to alleviate the obstacles needed to produce the change you want to see in that area.
- This *Din* is based on recognizing (the abilities of the believers that make up the Ummah) and facilitating for them the use of their respective gifts. Understand that if one person focuses upon an area that differs from your area of concern, he or she is complementing your work and not detracting from it by not joining you.
- Do not see other Muslims, whether organized groups or individuals, as competitors or antagonists. Rather, see them as brothers, and work with them or work separately with amicable relations, the least of which is giving the greetings with a smile.
- Inculcate good character as a practice and be courteous with Muslims and non-Muslims alike.
- Maintain excellent kinship bonds and forgive the shortcomings of your relatives for the sake of Allah in hopes that by doing so for His sake, He may forgive your shortcomings.
- Treat your wives with excellence, as a man is judged in this religion by how well he treats his wives and children.

- Ask Allah every day to purify your heart with the prayer of the Prophet related by Imam Ahmad and use the prayer for purification from hidden *shirk* three times in the morning and three times in the evening.
- Tithe some portion of your wealth on top of the *zakat* you pay. Commit to some Islamic cause financially and support it on a regular basis.
- Read the *Qur'an* in its entirety at least twice a year (At least once in *Ramadan* and once during the rest of the year. Try and read it with contemplation at least once a year).
- Commit to a serious practice of remembrance of Allah.
- Learn the rules of commanding good and forbidding evil before you attempt to do so as you may not realize all of the necessary ramifications to any given circumstance.
- Avoid judging and criticizing people and cultivate empathy and compassion in your heart for the creation of Allah.
- Pray everyday for your afflicted brothers and sisters through out the world, especially our defenseless women and children, that Allah gives us from His presence a protector *(khalifa)* and one who is victorious.
- Take care of your body.
- Make a sincere commitment to the *Din* of Allah and his Messenger every day of your life.
- Commit yourself to becoming a man or woman of taqwa
- Utilize your time. Do not allow the thief to steal this precious gift of time from you.
- Serve your Lord, then honor your parents, and treat all of the Muslims as brothers and sisters, the wayward and the wayfarers.

Hi-Tech Bedouins

By Javed Mohammed

What is a virtual community and why should you get sucked into one? How can we all be connected yet remain so isolated? Where do people live in communities where they chat without speaking, become intimate without touching, frown without making a face? Where can you hide with multiple identities yet show your identity to the whole world? Where can you make the least effort and get the most return? Who gets the loot and who's left holding the bag? When is more less? These are some of the many questions I would like to touch upon [in this chapter].

It's difficult to face the metaphorical tidal wave created by the explosion of technology that has been the earmark of the past 20 years. To live through such a period is to weather the eye of a hurricane and maintain balance during an earthquake. But that's what this little effort is about -- living in and being a part of the Information Revolution in Silicon Valley. When you're in the midst of a sea of change, observing the progression from the Mainframe, to the PC to the Internet, when long-standing principles are turned upside down, it makes you ponder and that is what these words are about. I'm going to turn the pause button on for a short time and just reflect on how we got here and possibly where we are heading?

As a Computer Engineering student at Manchester University (one of the founding institutions of the stored program computer) in the late 1970s, I was awed by the processing power of the supercomputer and the capacity of the disk-drive. After 11 years of design and architecture of Mainframe computers spanning three continents, my fate would take me into the marketing of semiconductors for the PC and now the technology for high-speed access to the Internet. Each technology was awesome in some way the variables being, speed, power, and complexity. And the more I learn, the less, in retrospect, I feel I know.

For those who think that the Internet Mania is something totally new, please rest assured that we have had many waves like this. Back in the seventeenth century, there was a Tulip Mania in Holland where the price of Tulips went nuclear much the same way hi-tech stocks have today. Those who borrowed to invest went bankrupt.

In the United States 200 years later, a similar speculative craze arose over the railroad industry, which was followed by an unhealthy interest in silver mining. Yes, there was a stock market frenzy in the 1920s during which people invested in companies of which they had no knowledge. Sound familiar? And yes there was a market "correction" that led to the crash, followed by the Great Depression. Fast forwarding to the sixties and we see the advent of the computer and then the birth of the PC. With each invention there was a hoard of companies that started. Thanks to the effects of market forces and consolidation only the strong survived.

Supposedly technology brings with it progress, but like many things in life it's a double-edged sword. We have eradicated many diseases and illnesses, and bore new ones. We have technology, which shrinks time to do any task, but nonetheless we seem to have less of it. We have developed and used nuclear power both to destroy life as in the case of nuclear weapons and to help give life as in radiation therapy for cancer.

However, progress, like beauty, lies in the eye of the beholder. Like many words we can give it the meaning we want, or take it as it's defined to us. As rational human beings we should always question and make a conscious decision in every step that impacts us, our families, our communities and our coming generations. Technology is not a magic wand that can overcome all our problems. At it's best it can help and compliment the God-given innate gifts we have. At it's worst it can dehumanize men and women, young and old, destroying the very fiber of our society.

I do not ask that you become a Luddite, dumping your high-tech toys. As a high-tech Bedouin, the next time you're in the store contemplating which gadget to add to your arsenal, think of the longevity of it. Each small, blazingly fast, shiny gizmo today will be a slow useless object tomorrow lying in a dump, waiting for it's half-life to come to an end.

Each new "monster" home or truck will add to the plethora of things that deplete the world of resources that are not being renewed at the rate that they are being consumed. A computer in every classroom or a cell-phone for every individual will not solve the social issues we have. The media in all their forms both directly in commercials and indirectly via content promote more than a product; they promote attitudes, values and lifestyles that surround consumption of that product. They send an implicit message about the standard of living and patterns of behavior that are a norm for the society. For the well-to-do, there's no issue. For the shrinking middle class and poor all over the world playing the constant game of catch-up, just trying to get on the accelerating treadmill of life becomes a self-defeating goal.

So let us pursue a livelihood of voluntary simplicity that directly contributes to the well being of the whole world and enables us to use more fully our innate capacities. The technology merry go round will continue turning; you just have to know when to get on and more importantly when to get off. With this I close as my cell-phone goes off. My voice-mail is full and I have so many emails to read. Maybe one day they will develop a technology that will take care of this generation of technology so that we can all have quality time, a meaningful life, and a real community. Until then, go slow, you Hi tech-Bedouins!

The Muslim Youth in America: Problems and Solution

by Maha Ezzeddine

Entrusted to generation after generation, the banner now lies in dusty battlefields, neglected and enshrouded with dust, guarded by only a few enduring soldiers. The once numerous trustees of the banner have struggled in countless battles against ignorance, corruption, and greed. The banner of which they are guardians flutters slightly, a witness to the masses who fled from its side to cower, in but a temporary refuge in the life of this world. Now, it is supported by a few exhausted hands and is protected by a mere handful.

Brothers and sisters, this banner is Islam, and we, the youth, are the next soldiers. In but a short time, Islam will be passed into our hands to protect, to preserve, and to fight for with the help of Allah. The banner of Islam glows with its light and sheds hope to the oppressed of this world. It is time for Islam to be carried throughout the world, into the remote corners of South America, through the narrow streets of Pakistan, through the war stricken villages of Bosnia, and into the frenzied bustle of New York, Chicago, and Washington. Yet, will we be worthy of such an honored trust? Are our ranks so firm with faith that the lofty banner will strike fear into the hearts of the army of Shaytaan? Or will we shrink from it and throw Islam aside at the first hint of difficulty? We must awaken to our impending responsibility and repair our gaping weaknesses so that our triumphant banner can be raised to new heights.

I can take up my pen to extol the accomplishments of the Muslim youth in America in the past two decades, comparing an almost undisturbed silence for many generations to a sudden burst of Islamic awareness. With as much ease, I can mourn our profound flows and gaze into the contorted future of Islam. The wisest road to take, however, is to adopt a middle route, neither contentment with our present situation nor hopelessness at our future. Through determination and much effort, we can conquer our weaknesses, with the help of Allah, and succeed.

Living in North America, we are assaulted from all sides by pitfalls and snares of this life. Numerous diseases seek to infect the beauty of walking on the straight path. We have been warned strongly against the vices of drugs, alcohol, peer pressure, and television. These problems are acknowledged by us all and every Muslim youth is aware of the countless temptations and difficulties he or she is forced to face every day. Yet, despite our awareness and preventive steps, there are no prominent attainments. Even though we are fully informed by the Qur'an and Sunnah of the thorns of this life, we still become entangled. In order to be the fortified wall that will protect ourselves from the furious waves of a disbelieving society, we must have a strong Islamic foundation and faith as enduring as stone. Perhaps, then, we should try a new approach and begin with the weaknesses that are birthed inside us.

The most conspicuous shortcoming I find in myself and others is a drastic scarcity of knowledge. We hope to be the guardians of a most noble religion, yet we know so little of it. We appeal to others to embrace it through our Dawah, yet little do we realize that we have not truly embraced it ourselves. At our fingertips lies a wealth of invaluable books and resources, such that is withheld from Muslims of some countries, yet we hesitate. Through knowledge of our religion, we can become spokesmen, rather than mere shadows of Islam. Knowledge should be the requirements from which we select the leaders of our youth. Instead we have mistakenly adopted the western standards with which to select our leaders, such as persuasiveness, charisma, and leadership. Though these are of benefit to any leader, the leaders of our youth require more than what worldly affairs require, and knowledge is surely a foremost determinant. Some of us have the zeal, the ability, and the will power to become new leaders in the light of Islam. However, our lack of Islamic knowledge sometimes impairs us and is as debilitating to our abilities as is the loss of sight.

I appeal, then, to myself and the thousands of American youth who truly posses a desire to serve Islam, to establish in ourselves a harmonious combination of wisdom, knowledge, and ambition. How many of us read not only read the Qur'an everyday, but also strive to understand it? Have any of us taken time out to memorize a few hadith and surahs? We must turn to the pages of our books and the halaqas of our scholars and learned ones so that we appreciate and realize the blessing of the gift of knowledge.

A second problem that threatens our Ummah so dangerously is our lack of piety. When we read the accounts of the Sahabah we should be moved to tears as we see the gaping fissure that lies between ourselves and them! How often do we find someone willing to give even a quarter of his or her savings for the sake of Allah as the companions so often did? Muslim dwellings often lay dark and silent throughout the night, rarely stirred by a fervent prayer. We tend to forget Allah as we step out of the gate of our Masjid and do not remember Him until our next prayer. How many of us, when we are sitting at a bus stop or taking notes in a classroom, actually whisper a few words of Dhikr? Surely the effort is trivial when we remember the reward!

Our purity of intention and piety also lay vulnerable to the insidious workings of pride. A watchful eye must be ever on the lookout inside ourselves for prayers best composed when in a congregation, money that is only given to charity in front of others, and a code of dress that is only observed in front of Muslims, for these are bold signs of an insincere heart.

Another predator that lies await for us in western society is that of affluence and self-indulgence. In the schools we are taught that we are "special" individuals. We become tricked into thinking that we are deserving of privileged rights and kingly treatment. We convince our parents to spend excessive amounts of money so that we can remain in fashion. We take money as something that originates from our own selves, and not as blessing endowed by Allah. Our free time becomes devoted to the pursuit of our own delight and pleasure, not realizing that this time is a gift. When we attend lectures and halaqas, we worry whether it will be interesting to our innovative minds or whether there will be any sports or refreshments. This egotism must stop. We must realize what lowly and humble creatures we are in the sight of Allah without our faith and love of Him. We could be cast out of our homes and be inflected by destitution were it not for His mercy

The final problem I will relate is the matter of priority.

Our neglect, lack of knowledge, and occupation with this world can be accredited to giving Islam a second place in our lives. It is easy to be caught up in this world; distracted by college decisions, school activities, sports, and scores. For those of us who attend Sunday school or other classes, why do we not pay as much attention to these matters as we do to those of public school or college? The youth should grant Islam the right of priority in all matters of their life. Our close friends should be chosen for their character, the Qur'an should be given its rightful part in our day, the masjid should be attended more often than the basketball court, and our thrill and pleasure should be found in working for Allah rather than in the odious company of a television. Only when we give our undivided attention to become the servants of Allah and His religion, will the brilliance of Islam be recognized. By repairing these internal cracks that weaken our Islamic resistance, we can resist the challenges American society hurls at us. By mending these weaknesses, we can become the capable reinforcements sent by Allah to lift the banner of Islam from under trampling feet and raise it in victory.

When we compare the youth of Islam to the youth of other peoples, we are pleased with what Islam has done to us. It has purified us from the majority of the both physical and mental poisons of this life. Alhamdulilah, we are not faced with the problems of murder or crimes among ourselves. Among us we have those who have surpassed American society's role models in sincerity of character and have become role models ourselves. We are at the top of a tower of society in terms of commitment to morals, devotion to family, and close knit communities. It is very easy, brothers and sisters, to breathe a sigh of relief when we are appreciated by the non-Muslims of American society for our values. Yet, do we dare slight our modern role models for the dazzling challenge of taking the Shahaba as our examples? For if we do, we slip down from our lofty level in modern society to an infinitely more humble level in the sight of Allah. In the stillness and darkness of our depth, we have only the tattered, yet exalted, be the first to take the banner and climb?

CONCLUSION

Some of you may be surprised to hear this, but in my youth, I had a whole fleet of planes. Alas, my dreams of becoming a pilot never came true; and yes, my empire has long gone. What took me to such meteoric heights? Well, it all started with my trips to the mosque. Each Sunday my father would give me eight pennies for bus fare between our home and the mosque. As I had a fascination with planes, I figured the only way I was going to get them was by saving. So I used to run three miles each way (nonstop, except for traffic lights) and save my bus fare. Every few weeks I was able to save enough to buy a plane. Eventually I had quite a collection of model fighter planes that I had assembled, as well as a deck that acted as my Aircraft carrier. My father, hearing of this, started to get concerned as he had other hopes for my career.

The reason I bring up this story, is that I find with children and the youth of today, the desire to have things. If I reflect back on my life, I find that many things that I accomplished (with God's help) and I feel proud of, came as the result of struggle. So although it's nice being able to take shortcuts some times, for most things in life, patience is not only a virtue but also a necessity. And it is this same patience that gives one contentment in times of trouble. As believers we should always be in a state of patience or gratitude as our most beloved Prophet (SAW) has taught us.

In this work there were several references to technology. In this Information Age, as we cross the millennium, there is no doubt that each succeeding generation will have at its disposal more information and will know more than the previous one. What really counts is how useful the information is. Once information bears relevance to our lives it becomes knowledge. When we can take the knowledge and learn when, where, and how to use it, it can become wisdom. Once we have wisdom and we execute on ideas, knowledge becomes action. So each stage of progression is a means to a transitory end. Although I refer to it in the text as knowledge, all I have done is share with you some information that I hope can bear some relevance to you, inspire you or just give you a new perspective.

I hope that having read the speeches and letters in this book you can look beyond the icons of the day as your role models.

In conclusion, as an individual who grew up as a first generation immigrant and who is now an immigrant raising a first generation, what are the major lessons that I have learned and would like to pass on?

First, I would like to say that at the dawn of this new millennium, living in Silicon Valley, this is an awesome time. Man's material accomplishments in the 21st century leave the times gone by in the dust. We have seen and faced both the Industrial and Information revolutions. As the speed of innovation increases, and creation of incredible amounts of wealth and power dawns upon us, there is a crying need that is not being fulfilled. What is this vacuum? It is a spiritual vacuum; one which has a spiritual lock whose key is faith.

Second, I hope that the higher education and knowledge we gain, whether it be in modern science, social science, religion, etc., guides us to the real wealth, which is success both in this world and the hereafter. I hope that we will seek to understand and apply Islam to the times that we live in; to meet the needs of our communities; that we liberate ourselves, so that wealth and power do not become our sole objects of human endeavor; that we do not blindly imitate everything that is in front of us, or reject everything around us, and lastly not to forget the value of the human touch for which there's no substitute.

Third, as ambassadors on earth we have to be the best of role models. In the example of the Prophet Muhammad (PBUH) we have a big responsibility to make sacrifices of time, wealth, skills, and whatever bounties God has blessed us with for the greater good of humanity. Start with your family, community and work outwards.

May God give you the vision, commitment, resources and time to use your abilities for a better cause, a better future, and a better humanity.

I close with these supplications from the Holy Qur'an:

"O my Lord and Sustainer!.
Grant me that I may be grateful for Your favor which You have bestowed upon me, and upon both my parents, and that I may work righteousness such as You may approve. And be gracious to me in my offspring. Truly, I have turned to You and truly I am of those who submit to You."

(46: 15)

"O my Lord and Sustainer! Bestow wisdom on me, and join me with the righteous.

(26:83)

"Our Lord and Sustainer! Let not our hearts deviate now after You have guided us, but grant us blessings and mercy from Your own presence, for You are the Grantor of boun ties without measure."

(3: 8)

(The supplications in the Qur'an and from the Prophet (PBUH) show us in the most beautiful and moving way possible what we should pray for and how. In fact there are du'aas of the Prophet for almost all occasions)

"O God, we seek Your help and ask Your forgiveness. We seek Your guidance and affirm our faith in You. We turn to You in repentance and put our trust in You. We give praise to You in the goodliest manner and offer our thanks to You and are not ungrateful to You...

"O God' You alone do we worship and unto You do we pray and prostrate ourselves. Towards You do we strive and hasten. We hope for Your mercy and dread Your chastisement. Indeed, Your chastisement shall overtake the disbelievers."

"O Lord! I seek Your protection against knowledge that profits not and a heart which fears not God and a mind that is not satisfied and a prayer that is not answered."

"O Lord' I beseech You for guidance, righteousness, chastity and self-sufficiency."

"O Lord! Direct me aright in my faith which is the guardian of my affairs and direct me aright in my life in which I have my being and set right my Hereafter which is my resort and make my life filled with every type of good and make my death a comfort from all ill."

Who is the Greatest of all Time?

Javed Mohammed

The answer depends on greatest at what, where, and in which time? There have been great prophets, nations, philosophers, kings and yes even athletes. Those who have stood the test of time excelled in several areas, overcame the biggest of tribulations, and persevered.

So who is greatest of all time? Without a hesitation, without a doubt it is the one and only God, Allah, Creator of the heavens and universe. Who are amongst the great Prophets? Adam, Abraham, Moses, Jesus and Muhammad (Peace be upon them all) and who amongst them is the greatest?
It is the last in the chain of the Prophets, Muhammad (Peace be upon him); a great Prophet, a just leader, the best husband, an outstanding father and the ideal role model for all humanity. Who is the greatest Caliph? It is Abu Bakr (RA) Who is the greatest military general, undefeated before and after Islam? It is Khalid Ibn Walid. Who is the greatest boxer of all time? One who could fight, float like a butterfly, sting like a bee, was handsome, a great poet? You know the answer to that one, Muhammad Ali.

So when posed the question who is the greatest?, one thing that becomes evident is that greatness comes from many dimensions of a person's life.

In this book are gems; gems of wisdom and gems of hope. A gems true value and beauty can only be appreciated by taking it out of the dark closet into the light. So I hope you can take the knowledge and wisdom between the covers of this book read, think and go and make a difference in the world. Use the Midas touch with everyone you come into contact with, that's the true heart of gold.

Remember life is full of challenges, some which may appear to be insurmountable, but perseverance and prayer are the keys to success. Muhammad Ali faced the most powerful of fighters from Sonny Liston, to George Foreman for the World Heavy Weight Championship. Against Foreman, Ali was told that he didn't have a chance, that he didn't have a prayer as Foreman had annihilated all his previous challengers. His response was "all I need is a prayer, because if that prayer reaches the right man, not only will George Foreman fall but mountains will fall!" Muhammad Ali won the World Heavy Weight Championship three times each time using a different strategy and always coming from a position of strength, his strength and of course by Allah's mercy. I bring this up not to promote boxing, but just to give another of so many examples we can look at, where the odds may appear to be against you, but with courage, determination, and prayers, the odds become insignificant.

You cannot compete with others unless you are coming from a position of strength. In order for you to know your strength as an individual, a community, and a nation you must as in the words of Malcolm X, "form the habit of learning how to see things for yourself, listen for yourself and think for yourself; then you are in a better position to judge for yourself."

In order for you to go down this path, you must know your history, your beliefs and values. Who are your heroes and rolemodels? This book is but a small endeavor in that direction. Once you know who you really are and what you're about in Allah's creation, you can start to make a difference.

I encourage you to be constantly asking yourselves, what is the best use of my time? What is the best use of my "wealth? And what is the best use of the knowledge and talents God has blessed me with?" Don't waste your time in endless discussions about problems you cannot influence. As an old Arab saying goes, "the action of one person which affects a thousand people is better than the talk of a thousand people which affects one person." So leverage your God-given gifts to benefit as many people as you can.

Be an optimist, but also be pragmatic. We all know strength lies in unity. So leave the discussions of uniting nations, lets start by focussing on uniting our families and communities. Remember, it's easy to point a finger at others, but with that same hand you have the three fingers pointing at you. In most situations we are in violent agreement about our objectives. So don't let petty things get magnified, don't let your egos get in the way for what's better for the greater good. Just as in the most intimate of relationships of husband and wife, parent and child there's give and take, we overlook each others faults for harmony, then we need to continue down this path with others whose our lives touch.

Although it's a cliché, there is a reality to it. The more things change, the less they change. We can see this in technology, fashion, tastes, and other aspects of life. Of course we need to live and learn to thrive in the times that we live in, but if what society teaches us is to chase a moving target, then we will only tire ourselves out in trying to reach this virtual utopia of life. This reminds me of the story of two men, one who says to the other lets have a race. The other asks to where, to which the first replies to the red stoplight.

So the race starts and the first guy returns after a few minutes. The second guy is nowhere to be seen and is lost for several days. When they finally meet up, the person who made the suggestion asked his friend what happened to him. His reply was that he started chasing the light, which kept moving further and further away. He ended up chasing the tail light of a car. So ask yourself, what are you chasing after?

The future belongs to those who are rich not in material things but morals, not in technical wizardry but spiritual fulfillment, not those who take the most but those who give the most.

So in conclusion, Who is the greatest of all time? It is Allah and Allah knows best!

Analysis of Speeches

Many of the speeches given by famous orators are covered in books and of later times on audio and/or videotape. We hear a great speech, but we don't know what makes it so. What follows are the analysis of some of the major speeches given in the previous text in Chapter three.

I am not a linguist, so my objective is not to present a detailed analysis of each speech, but to see what made it great and what are the common threads.

Analysis of Prophet Muhammad's Last Sermon

The Prophet (Peace Be Upon Him, PBUH) last sermon is a very powerful and concise message of his mission to all of humanity. The message starts off by opening up to all people *"O People".* This term is used several times in the sermon, making use of parallelism and in turn building a certain rhythm. As the original speech was given in Arabic, of course there is no way the true style and content can be accurately portrayed in English. However, the message is so important and for those of us whose primary language is English I will continue.

The opening is an attention-getter, where the attention is obtained explicitly (lend me an attentive ear and listen to what I am saying to you carefully) and implicitly. Fourteen hundred years ago there was no media to broadcast the message, so the Prophet (PBUH) asked for the message to be passed on by word-of-mouth *"take these words to those who could not be present here today."* For emphasis the next statement uses parallelism and strikes a chord with the listener, building of what he (or she) believes. *"O People, just as you regard this month, this day, this city as Sacred"* Reciprocity is used in several places "Hurt no one so that no one may hurt you", "you have certain rights with regard to your women, but they also have right over you".

Next, the central pillars of Islam are mentioned,

"worship ALLAH, say your five daily prayers (Salah), fast during the month of Ramadhan, and give your wealth in Zakat. Perform Hajj". As we proceed through the sermon we can see it's comprehensiveness, both in the rights and obligations of humanity to God and also to other humans.

Another technique used is to repeat a message, but in a different way, e.g. to get the attention *""O People, lend me an attentive ear"* is used first, then half way through again to make sure the attention remains *"O People, listen to me in earnest"*

In the conclusion, we are reminded of discharging our duties and closing in God's name. *"Be my witness O Allah that I have conveyed your message to your people."*

Analysis of the Letter of Prophet Muhammad to Negus, King of Ethiopia

The Prophet Muhammad (PBUH) sent this letter to the King of Ethiopia when the Meccan rulers were oppressing the early Muslims. The letter is as most of the communication of the Prophet (PBUH), brief. It starts by praising Allah and immediately starts to build rapport. The source of rapport is the common belief in Jesus by the Christians and the Muslims. The letter then goes onto a brief introduction of the Prophet (PBUH), and the purpose of his message. It concludes by the call to action both in terms of accepting the message of Prophethood and the help requested for the first group of emigrants.

Analysis of Abu Bakr's Inauguration Speech

Compared to most presidential inaugurations, we see that this speech is extremely short. It starts in humility, (I am not the best of you) and ends in humility, (I am only human, so make allowance for me). An interesting parallel with a twist is used, which not only captures the attention, but forces the listener to think (considering weak as strong and vice versa). Next, he outlines where his policy will come from (no innovation and following the Prophet SAW) and the criteria of when the people should follow him (if I do well assist me! and if I deviate, straighten me out), something unheard of in this era from any leader.

Next a series of three admonitions: And reckon with yourselves before you are taken to reckoning! No people ever abandoned jihad (struggle) in the way of Allah except that Allah afflicted them with disgrace (i.e. don't abandon jihad) And never did an obscenity appear among people except that Allah caused disaster to spread among them (avoid obscenity). Space repetition is used again regarding obedience, (Then obey me as long as I obey Allah).

In conclusion, he again states that he is taking on the role of Caliph and leadership reluctantly. In all, a very concise and powerful speech.

Gold

Analysis of Letter From Mecca: Malcolm X

Malcolm's letter starts with a strong expression of emotion, which immediately captivates the reader. " Never have I witnessed such overwhelming spirit of hospitality and true brotherhood." It then goes on to set the context and the universal appeal of the message "as is practiced by people of all colors and races here in this ancient Holy Land, the home of Abraham, Muhammad, and all the other Prophets of the Holy Scriptures." Malcolm gets you in the picture by using imagery, "There were tens of thousands of pilgrims, from all over the world"

Later a feeling of suspense and emotion is used to engage the reader with the phrase, "You may be shocked by these words coming from me".

Malcolm used a lot of parallelism in his speeches and this letter is no exception. "I have eaten from the same plate, drunk from the same glass, and slept in the same bed (or on the same rug) -- while praying to the same God". Here it is the sameness, same plate, same glass, same God that is used. Others that are used through out the speech are, "white from their minds, the white from their behavior, and the white from their attitude.

Contrasting is used in the following example, "And in the words and in the actions and in the deeds of the "white" Muslims; I felt the same sincerity that I felt among the black African. "The people are now given an identity as to where they are from; "the black African Muslims of Nigeria, Sudan, and Ghana".

It then draws on the analogies of the Oneness of God, and the Oneness of Man; "I could see from this, that perhaps if white Americans could accept the Oneness of God, then perhaps, too, they could accept in reality the Oneness of Man". Another analogy, which gets the attention of the reader, is by comparing racism to cancer, "With racism plaguing America like an incurable cancer". A sense of urgency is then brought to the message "Perhaps it could be in time to save America from imminent disaster." It is compared with an event which people do not want ever to be repeated; "the same destruction brought upon Germany by racism that eventually destroyed the Germans themselves"

Finally, in his conclusion Malcolm draws on his personal experience in the way he was treated again using parallelism and the same pattern that he started with to end the speech. "Never have I been so highly honored. Never have I been made to feel more humble,... Never would I have ever thought of dreaming that I would ever be a recipient of such honor's honors that in America would be bestowed upon a King, not a Negro". The concluding statement is a short prayer; "All praise is due to Allah, the Lord of all the Worlds."

Success Factors of Great Speeches

The speeches and examples that were included in the text have common principles, including brevity, effective use of words, and powerful introduction and conclusions. This appendix explains some of the principles behind what makes an effective speech.

Starting Off

The beginnings of these speeches capture the attention of the audience using one of the following principles.

1. Referring to the subject or occasion
2. Addressing the audience directly
3. Asking a rhetorical question
4. Making a startling statement of fact or opinion
5. A strong expression of emotion

The Main Points

Brevity, vividness, relevance, and parallelism are four characteristics of good phrasing which were used in the speeches.

Brevity

Both in the address of the Prophet Muhammed (PBUH) and Abu Bakr (RA), we see a lot is said with very few words. This conciseness gives the message as briefly as possible without distorting the meaning so it is easy to grasp. It has a single clear objective with some form of a memorable hook. Brevity is a simple word, but in reality it is a very challenging concept to put into practice. Generally speaking the shorter the time available to get the message means more time spent in preparing that message

The following is a law of speeches, which I hope you'll like:

> • "The time to prepare for a speech is directly proportional to the importance of the speech and inversely proportional to the time available to get the message across."
>
> •Javed Mohammed's Law of Speeches

Vividness

The speeches state the main points in attention provoking, lively words, and phrases. They make effective use of words using language which is accurate, simple, appropriate and use imagery. Concrete and specific words are used for accuracy and simple short words and phrases are used so that the simplest of people can understand them. Examples and analogies are used that bear relevance to the time and place of the people. Imagery using the senses of sight, smell, hearing, taste, and touch are effectively used.

Relevance

In the speeches the main points are worded so they appeal to the interests and concerns of listeners; they use one of the following principles of analogy, illustration or facts.

1. Analogies are used in the Holy Quran and in the sayings of the Prophet (PBUH) for comparison. They point out the similarities between something which is known, understood, or believed and something which is not. An example of this is the letter of Prophet Muhammad (PBUH) to the Ethiopian King, where the likeness of Jesus (PBUH) is compared to that of Adam (PBUH) to show

that both were human beings.

2. Illustrations are expanded examples, presented in a narrative form and having about them some striking or memorable quality. Illustrations tells a story which has happened, could have happened or probably will happen. Again there are many example of this in the Holy Quran.
3. Facts: (e.g. Testimony/Statistics) Citing verbatim the opinions or conclusions of others. The purpose is to add weight or impressiveness to an idea or to supply proof of point.

Parallelism

Several of the speeches use a uniform type of sentence structure, e.g. in the Prophet's last sermon "O People,..." is used several times and similar phraseology in stating main points. They use prepositions, connectives, and verb forms which permit a similar balance, rhythm, and direction of thought

Ending

The endings (or conclusion) of these speeches focus the thought of the audience on the central theme and purpose using one of the following principles:

1. Issuing a challenge or call to action
2. Summarizing
3. Restatement: Reiteration of the key message(s) in different words.
4. Asking a question and then answering it or leaving audience to ponder on it
5. Supplying an additional incentive to belief or action[11]

Teachers Guide

The text in this book may be used to explore communication in various forms from quotes, speeches, letters and essays. It can be used both by individuals for self-growth as well as in a more formal learning environment.

It is targeted for the youth, so it can be used with middle, high school, and college-age students. Following are some ideas on exercises that can be conducted using the text.

1. Split up the class to focus on different sections of the book.
2. Have them read, discuss and present what they learn from the lessons in life of others. What is relevant to them and how can they apply it to their lives.
3. Have each student select three of their favorite quotes and one speech. Allow each two to five minutes to discuss why they made their selection.
4. Have each student select a speech, letter, or essay and have them read it with the energy and enthusiasm as close as they can to the original.
5. Select speeches (including letters or essays) or have students select them, and have them discuss what makes the speech inspirational. Use the Analysis in the back of the text as discussion points.
6. Have students read the text and discuss what it means to them about the culture, the history of that time and how it could relate to the present.
7. After reading text and discussing it, have students develop their own inspirational speeches, letters, or essays which they would like to deliver at an auspicious

occasion. Make it competitive.

8. Use videotapes to supplement text to learn more about contemporary figures like Muhammad Ali and Malcolm X to discuss their communication styles.
9. Based on interest of students have them research their favorite "role-model" to learn about what those people stood for. Have them write an essay and/or deliver a presentation on the subject.
10. Get students to comment and/or critique the book by placing their comments on Amazon.com, barnesandnoble.com or do a book review for a local newspaper.
11. Have students interview their parents and relatives and get them to share their most important lessons in life.
12. Discuss them in class, have each student set up goals or commitments based on them, send them to the author at gems1_us@yahoo.com
13. Conduct an authors forum. Invite this and other authors to discuss the authoring, publishing experience.

The Art of Speech

Chapter three brought together speeches and letters with depth and breadth for us all to ponder. How can we use inspirational material like this to address an audience? The following is an example of how you can leverage of great orators, scholars, and the like.

Once in a while, we may be asked or find ourselves having to say some words of wisdom at a social event. When my younger sister was going to get married in Manchester, England, I wanted to "connect " with primarily a Muslim audience. However, there were people of other faiths including Christian and Hindu. I had heard an excellent sermon given by Dr. Khalid Siddiqui from San Jose at a friends wedding in Fresno. I was able to get the video tape and transcribe a couple of key points. Similarly I have heard Imam Siraj Wahaj from Brooklyn New York, give some inspiring Friday sermons on the status of woman in Islam and her origin from Adam (a belief shared in the Bible). Again, I took the arduous task of transcribing some of the key points. Now trying to combine two totally different speeches with speckles from myself proved a daunting task.

Having gotten the material for the body of the speech, I moved onto working on the introduction and conclusion. I wanted to capture the attention of the audience so I chose to use the "shock" treatment. Once again, I had heard Imam Siraj use this in another of his sermons, "It has been said that the enemy will not teach you the art of three things" Who is the enemy was a captivating thought. I chose to make three major points and use the "three tell thems", "Today I would like to share with you how Islam views marriage. I will do this by explaining the relationship between man and woman, then between husband and wife, and finally talking about setting expectations. How we can have happier and long lasting marriages?"

I then quoted from the Quran a verse, which would be very familiar turf not only to Muslims but Christians as well.

"O mankind fear your Lord who created you from a single soul (Adam) and from it created it's mate (Hawaii or Eve) and from them spread many men and women (because one of the purposes of life is the continuation of life).
Fear Allah, in Whom you claim the rights of one another and towards the wombs that bore you. Surely Allah watches over you"

The explanation of this followed. The second major point related to the relationship between man and woman. For this once again there was a quote from the Holy Quran. This gives an analogy we are all familiar with, clothes and how they cover and protect us. The relationship between husband and wife is explained in a beautiful verse of the Quran

"They your wives are a garment (dress, libaas) for you and you are a garment for them"

The third and last point I chose to make was regarding setting expectations. Here I went on limb and as I was flying from San Francisco to Manchester, I chose the analogy of flying and how a marriage just like a plane ride can experience turbulence, so it was very important to buckle up.

I then reiterated a summary of the three key points (tell

them what you told them) and wanted a powerful conclusion. Here I used some parallelism (If you want...) and tied it in to the introduction. Last, but not least, I wanted to show the universal message of Islam and made a broad general statement about our objective in life.

"Today I have touched on the tip of an iceberg. If you want learn the art of warfare study the Quran and Sunnah. If you want learn the art of self sufficiency study the Quran and Sunnah. If you want learn the art of marriage study the Quran and Sunnah. Only by doing this can we rise up to being the best of creation and being the Ambassadors on planet Earth."

After reviewing and revising the speech many times over, things started to fall into place. However, I wanted to say a lot, even by cutting it down I was down to 15 minutes. When I read the speech to my family they asked to me to reduce it even further to ten minutes. So the following is what I ended up giving, and yes it was very well received.

The Art of Marriage

(Composed by Javed Mohammed, content from Dr. Khalid Siddiqui and Imam Siraj Wahaj)

I begin in the name of Allah the Compassionate the Merciful. Praise be to Allah. We praise him and request His help and ask his forgiveness. And we seek refuge in Allah from the evil of our souls and the mischief of our deeds. Whoever Allah guides will never go astray and whomever Allah allows to go astray, there is no one to guide them. I bear witness there is no Lord worthy of worship except Allah (SWAT) alone and I bear witness that Muhammed (SAW) was His servant and Messenger.

It has been said that the enemy will not teach you the art of three things: The art of warfare, the art of self-sufficiency, and the art of marriage. The enemy will not want you to learn the art of warfare, because they are afraid you may defeat them. They will not want you to know the art of self-sufficiency because they want you to remain dependent on them. Why would the enemy not want you to know the art of Marriage?

I think it stems from the fact that an unstable marriage leads to an unstable family, and an unstable family leads to an unstable community, and an unstable community leads to an unstable nation. But we are blessed to be Muslims, and Islam is the religion of stability.

Today I would like to share with you how Islam views marriage. I will do this by explaining the relationship between man and woman, then between husband and wife, and finally talking about setting expectations. How we can have happier and long lasting marriages?

(PART 1)

The Quran says:
"O mankind fear your Lord who created you from a single soul (Adam) and from it created it's mate (Hawa or Eve) and from them spread many men and women (because one of the purposes of life is the continuation of life).
Fear Allah, in Whom you claim the rights of one another and towards the wombs that bore you. Surely Allah watches over you"

This Address is to the whole of humanity. It says that two people can only come and live together by saying that in the name of the Creator we say yes to life, yes to responsibility, yes to living together as deputies on Earth.

The purpose of life is to gain the pleasure of Allah (SWAT) by being a kind, helpful and loving member of human society. In order to do this we need to create the consciousness of God. The verses conclude by saying that "don't forget, God is watching you."

To understand these verses let us take a look at a Hadith of the Prophet (SAW): "Act kindly towards women, for they were created from the rib, and the most curved part of a rib is it's upper part, if you attempt to straighten it you will break it and if you leave it alone it will remain curved, so act kindly towards women. "This Hadith deals with interpersonal relationship. Some things to understand from this hadith are: As woman was created from the rib, a man is incomplete without a woman and woman is incomplete without a man. The nature of man and woman complement each other. If we understand and accept this it will lead to happiness, rather than the competing forces that we see in Western society.

The hadith shows us that the woman is curved both

physically and spiritually. This is what gives her, her beauty and makes her attractive to the man. The hadith then concludes by saying that, if man attempts to reshape and remold the woman into his own image by trying to straighten her, he will break her and breaking her means divorcing her. Of all the permitted things, the thing which is most hated to Allah is divorce, so we must avoid it at all costs.

(PART 2)

The relationship between husband and wife is explained in a beautiful verse of the Quran "They your wives are a garment (dress, libaas) for you and you are a garment for them."

The libaas (dress) is the closest thing to our bodies and husband and wife are instructed to become close to each other. The clothes on our bodies serve three purposes:

1. Clothes provide protection from the heat and cold and in a like manner husband and wife must become the protectors of each other.
2. Clothes cover our bodies (including scars and any blackspots) and in a like manner husband and wife must cover the faults of each other, as it is Allah alone who is perfect.
3. Clothes, especially beautiful clothes present us in the most beautiful way and in a like manner husband and wife must speak to each other with respect, humility, and beautiful words about each other.

So never forget this, especially in moments of hardship and dispute. This is why the Prophet (SAW) has told us time and time again to act kindly towards women.

(PART 3)

Let us now move onto setting expectations. The best analogy of a marriage taking place is that of a plane standing on the runway with bride, bridegroom, families and community. As the plane takes off, it will level of at an altitude like 30,000 feet. As it proceeds on its journey, it will hit some turbulence. When the plane starts to shake like this, the captain will ask you to fasten your seatbelt. As the plane proceeds further on its journey, it may hit a lot of turbulence.

Actually a British Airways 747 was flying past Mount St. Helens after it had erupted. The ash caused all four engines to fail and the plane fell 20,000 feet. Can you imagine what was going through the minds of those people? Imagine if someone had gone for the emergency exit, not only would they have got sucked out, they would have put in jeopardy the life of all the passengers. So it is in marriage, like turbulence conflict is inevitable in a marriage, but it is the ability to resolve conflict which makes marriages last.

In my conclusion, we have talked about the relationship between man and woman. How woman was created from the rib and how man needs to be careful in how he treats woman because of her emotional makeup. We have talked about the relationship between husband and wife, and how each is a garment for the other and needs to protect, cover, and beautify each other with gentle words. We talked about setting expectations and I gave the example of the Airplane and turbulence, how conflict is inevitable in a marriage, but it is the ability to resolve conflict which makes marriages last. Today, I have touched on the tip of an iceberg.

If you want to learn the art of warfare study the Quran and Sunnah. If you want to learn the art of self sufficiency study the Quran and Sunnah. And If you want to learn the art of marriage, study the Quran and Sunnah. Only by doing this can we rise up to being the best of creation and being the Ambassadors on planet Earth.

May Allah bless this marriage. If I have made any mistakes they are my mistakes alone, and if there is any goodness in what has been said, then all praise is due to Allah. Thank you. Assalamu alikum.

(P.S. The explanation about the verses from the Quran is taken from a khutbah by Dr. Khalid Siddiqui of San Jose, CA and the explanation about the hadith of the curved rib is taken from a khutbah by Imam Siraj Wahaj of New York, NY).

Gold

A

Aayah: A sign, a verse from the Quran
Adab: Manners, etiquette
Allah: Arabic word for the One and only True God, Creator and Sustainer of all creation
Allahu Akbar: God is most Great
Alhamdulilah: All Praise is due to God, phrase used by Muslims in all situations in life
Amal: Action
Amanah: Trust, responsibility
As-salaamu alaykum: Islamic greeting meaning peace be upon you

D

Dawa: Invitation to Islam
Deen, Din: Simple translation is Religion, but encompasses a way of life
Dua'a: Supplication (prayer), calling upon God

H

Hadith: Saying of the noble Prophet
Hajj: Pilgrimage to Mecca, 5th pillar of Islam and compulsory on all adult Muslims who are able to go
Halaal: Permissible
Haram: Unlawful, Prohibited
Hikmah: Wisdom

I

Ibaadah: Worship
Imaam: Leader
Insha Allah: God willing
Isa: Arabic name of Jesus (PBUH)

J

Jihaad: Striving in the cause of Allah
Jannah: Paradise

K

Kabah: Cube shaped building in Mecca, which is the first house of worship built for mankind
Khalifah: Caliphate
Khutbah: Sermon

M

Mariam: Arabic name of Virgin Mary
Masjid: A place of prostration, a mosque
Muslim: One who submits to or obeys the laws of God

N

Nasihah: Sincere advice
Niyyah: Intention

P

PBUH: Peace Be Upon Him, said after the name of the Prophet(s)

Q

Qibla: The direction of Makkah

Qiyam: Standing at night in prayer
Qur'an: Holy book revealed to Prophet
Muhammed(SAW).
Source of guidance for Muslims. Preserved, memorized,
and
unchanged since revelation

R

RA: Radiya Allah Anhu, may Allah accept his actions
Rab: Lord and Sustainer
Ramadan: Month of fasting and pillar of Islam
Rizq: Sustenance

S

Sabr: Patience
Sadaqah: Charity
Sahabah: Companions of the Prophet (PBUH)
SWT, SWAT: Subhana WatAllah, used after the name of
Allah
SAW: Salla Allahu Alayhi wa Salaam, may Allah's peace and
blessings be upon the Prophet
Salaat, Salah: Prayer and pillar of Islam. There are five
obligatory
prayers per day
Sawm, Siyam: fasting in month of Ramadan
Shahadah: Bearing witness there is no God but Allah
(SWT) and
Muhammad (SAW) is his Messenger
Shura: Mutual consultation
Shariah: The moral and legal code of Islam
Shirk: Associating others in worship with God (the only
Sin which won't be forgiven) according to the Quran

Sunnah: Path or example, refers in particular to the examples of the Prophet Muhammad (SAW) and includes what he said, what he did and what he agreed to.

T

Tawhid: Belief in the oneness of Allah (SWT)

U

Ummah: Community or nation

Z

Zakat, Zakah: Obligatory sharing of wealth with needy, a pillar of Islam

About the Author

Javed Mohammed, a marketing manager and ex-engineer in Silicon Valley's hi-tech industry, has written several community based booklets based on his experiences at Mecca for the Pilgrimage, the Job Search, and remodeling a house, which have been well received. He has acted as both host and producer of a Cable-TV show covering Islamic news and views. He is an accomplished public speaker having presented at various conferences and local schools addressing both teachers and students.

Permissions

1 (p44) Sacrifice, excerpt from "The Making of a Muslim" by permission of the Islamic Foundation. ©

2 (pp57-59) " The sayings of Imam Ali (RA)" from, Living and Dying with Grace, translated by Thomas Cleary, © 1995. Reprinted by arrangement with Shambhala Publications, Inc., Boston, www.shambhala.com"

3 (pp78-86) "Has the Prayer Lost its Power?", reprinted from "Let us be Muslims" by permission of The Islamic Foundation, © Markfield Dawah Center, Ratby Lane, Markfield, Leicester LE67 9RN, United Kingdom

4 (pp87-90) "Letter from Mecca" from The Autobiography of Malcolm X with Alex Haley
Copyright © 1964 by Alex Haley and Malcolm X
Copyright © 1965 by Alex Haley and Betty Shabazz

5 (pp91-93) "Me...We by Muhammad Ali", reprinted by Permission of Forbes Magazine © 1999 Forbes 1999

6 (pp96-97) "Agenda for changing or condition" by Hamza Yusuf, reprinted by permission from Zaytuna Institute, www.zaytuna.org

7 (pp102-107) "The Muslim Youth in America", reprinted by Permission of The Message magazine, 166-26 89th Ave., Jamaica, NY 11432-4254 © 1998

References

[1] Adapted from, Hold Fast Your Dreams by Carrie Boyko and Kimberly Colen (pp33-34)

[2] Life's Little Instruction Book by H. Jackson Brown Jr

[3] Holy Qur'an: Surah Luqman 12-19, Translated by Abdullah Yusuf Ali.

[4] Letters of the Holy Prophet by Sultan Ahmad Qureshi

[5] The Sayings and Wisdom of Imam Ali (RA) by the Muhammadi Trust, Zahra Publications.

[6] Training Guide For Islamic Workers P59 (Kanz al 'Ummal III 130-135)

[7] Islam in Andalus by Ahmad Thomson and Muhammad Ata ur-Rahman P14-16

[8] The Cultural Atlas of Islam by Ismail Farooqi and Lois Farooqi P215-216 Al Futuhat

[9] Referenced from USA Today, December 10, 1999

[10] Islam the Natural Way by Abdul Wahid Hamid

[11] Adapted from Principles of Speech Communication by Monroe & Ehninger

Index